A VIEW
from the
INLAND
NORTHWEST

Everyday Life in America

STEPHEN J. LYONS

GUILFORD, CONNECTICUT

*For my mother,
who gave me words, wisdom,
and wings*

Text design by M.A. Dubé
Map by Stefanie Ward

Library of Congress Cataloging-in-Publication Data
Lyons, Stephen J.
    A view from the Inland Northwest: everyday life in America / Stephen J. Lyons.
        p. cm.
ISBN 0-7627-3052-8
    1. Inland Empire—Description and travel. 2. Inland Empire—Social life and customs. 3. Idaho—Description and travel. 4. Idaho—Social life and customs. 5. Washington (State)—Description and travel. 6. Washington (State)—Social life and customs. 7. Lyons, Stephen J.—Travel—Idaho. 8. Lyons, Stephen J.—Travel—Washington (State) I. Title.
F750.L96 2004
979.5'043—do22

                                                                    2004051044

Manufactured in the United States of America
First Edition/First Printing

CONTENTS

ACKNOWLEDGMENTS

T HIS BOOK IS FOR MY FAMILY and in loving memory of Seymour Goldberg and Charles Uchytil.

I am forever indebted to the many people who trusted me with their personal stories. I am especially thankful to Ben Benthien, Rei Osaki, and Etta Wegner. Gratitude to Rose for allowing me to write about her (again!).

Sincere appreciation to Dad and Rob for their continued support. Keep the honey coming.

Some of these writings appeared in various forms in *Hope, Writers on the Range,* the *Sun,* and *Northern Lights.* The following editors of these publications are tireless advocates for writers: Amy Rawe, Jon Wilson, Paul Larmer, Betsy Marston, Andrew Snee, Sy Safransky, and Deb Clow.

Many thanks to Mary Norris at Globe Pequot for choosing me.

I am grateful for the friendship of Ken Olsen, and for my Durango family. Love and whiskers to Betty Jean.

My occasional office assistants Toby and Mickey were especially helpful. A generous fellowship from the Illinois Arts Council made this project easier.

Without the support of my wife, Jan Ellen Engel Gantz, I would never have the time and space in which to write. Her love is more than I could have ever imagined. "Every moment counts, every good act is a success, and the world is ours to behold."

INTRODUCTION

IN A MUSTY CABIN DEEP IN THE HEART of Idaho's wilderness, I once sat on an old metal-framed bed during a spectacular evening thunderstorm and read Zane Grey's *Desert of Wheat* by flickering kerosene light. Overhead, a family of pack rats scuffled within a crawl space, sprinkling dust and insulation across my chest. As the eye of the storm passed over the cabin, the rats' movements intensified to a frantic dance. Outside, the dark forest lit up just before each atmospheric explosion. Lightning collided with ancient stone and wood. Rain battered the tin roof. The kerosene ran out. Across Big Creek, a herd of elk stumbled hurriedly across a talus slope. I couldn't stop listening. My ears were never so acutely tuned. I thought I could hear individual twigs fall in the rain and the bounding leaps of mule deer as they rushed toward dry ground. I never wanted the night to end.

Earlier that summer day, I had hiked the few miles down the creek to its confluence with the Salmon River. Native cutthroat trout—which hatcheries will never duplicate—rose and dove at my feet. As happens any time I walk alone in the woods, my senses took on an acuity usually never required for this modern life. Sharp smells of pine mixed with a hint of what I swear suggested cinnamon and wet dirt. My bad eyesight sharpened, and I saw every crease and crevice of my surroundings. With the wonderful exception of a set of Native American pictographs depicting bighorn sheep and their hunters, the area was devoid of any stain of humanity. I have rarely felt such joy.

Rare is the time when we can quiet our inquisitive minds sufficiently and enjoy the present tense. Rarer still is knowing which quick hours in a long life will be the kind of precious touchstones we will draw on later in life. Indeed, as I somehow intuitively knew then, I never did return to Big Creek. Most likely I never will. During my most generous reflections I admit that even that one magical night is an underserved gift. Just about every other second I wish I were back in the cabin—Zane Grey novel and rats included.

❧ ❦

As I BEGAN TO ASSEMBLE THIS BOOK of personal essays and narrative journalism, I recalled other one-of-a-kind moments that occurred in the region of northern Idaho and eastern Washington I am calling "the Inland Northwest." You will read about sandhill cranes, wolves, great horned owlets, migrating turkey vultures, and white-faced ibises, the imaginary blue falcon and a hundred-year flood. With the modern age encroaching from all directions, those few encounters with the natural world take on an even greater meaning for me than simple nostalgia. I see them as a secret path to a textured reality, to a place where I feel safe and sane. I will always seek them out, echoing what poet Mary Oliver once wrote, "I don't want to end up simply having visited this world."

Besides the overwhelming pulse of nature—much of it beleaguered and denuded in this part of the West—I also set out to find people with that feisty combination of fierce independence and undying awareness of their environment that typifies this region. I was lucky in that regard, meeting men and women who, like salmon swimming against the current, hold on to a textured life. One of those gifts is Etta Wegner, the artist who has lived for eight decades in the bluffs above the Snake River in Washington's Whitman County. From the time that she was a young girl rescuing injured animals, she has trained her eye to look for the quiet miracles in the curvy eyebrow places, the old growth hawthorns, and overhead in the thermals. The results are precious drawings of birds, including her beloved, the elusive California quail. My favorite sits on my writing desk: a trio of baby barn owls.

She once wrote to me of discovering an egg-shaped stone nestled perfectly in another rock near the top of the Bitterroot Mountains some fifty years ago. Even after half a century, her excitement still sparkled: "It was so obvious that it had to be the result of rushing water spinning in it for hundreds of years. It was awesome."

Etta left the rocks undisturbed. She could not bring herself to break up such perfect geologic symmetry.

Her stories, and all the ones in this book, are like that electric night of thunder and lightning I experienced in the Idaho mountains. Unexpected gifts. Now I offer them to you.

FIRST, AN INFORMAL GEOGRAPHY LESSON IS IN ORDER. The region in the book has four fluctuating borders that defy political boundaries. To the north, stay just below the Canadian border, somewhere around Bonners Ferry, Idaho, or the lake country of Coeur d'Alene and the nearby mining remnants of the Silver Valley, around Wallace. To the south, there is no reason to go any farther than the narrow Salmon River canyons that surround Riggins, a town that a not-too-secret band of aging secessionists say will be the capital of an imagined future state called "North Idaho." (They are quite willing to turn over Boise, the actual capital, to Utah, Nevada, and Oregon, even France: all offers and trades considered.) If you have a vehicle with trusty brakes, be sure to drive the switchbacks up to the Seven Devils Wilderness Area. Or you can walk: about 20 miles up hill. From the highest peaks, look across Snake River's Hell's Canyon at Oregon's Wallowa Mountains. Beyond that range is Malheur National Wildlife Refuge, an area worthy of a lifetime's study.

As one travels east, the boundary to this book blurs. To stay true to the idea of keeping to the sunset side of the Continental Divide, you could stop in tiny Elk River, Idaho, then negotiate what passes for a road across Dworshak Dam into Orofino. From there, if you were so inclined, you might climb up onto the bluffs above the Clearwater River, past Grangemont into Pierce or Headquarters. In any case, make sure you have plenty of gas and some tread left on your tires. A satellite phone might be handy, too. Tell someone where you are going and your estimated time of return. Or not.

Moving west, drive Washington State Highway 26 from Colfax, Washington, and marvel at the transition from wheat and pea fields to the scoured scablands around Washtucna and Kahlotus. If you love basalt formations, this will be your kind of place. Look closely at the cliffs, and you may see a barn owl or the evidence of the Missoula Flood.

Keeping all of the above in mind, do not pass up Kamiak Butte, the Blue Mountains, the Grand Coulee, White Pine Drive, Palouse Falls, or Potholes Reservoir. And a thousand other places.

Another way to grasp the geography is to consult as I do the 1994 edition of DeLorme's *North America Atlas and Gazetteer.* Tear out page 15. (It's the only one you will need.) Set aside a decade or two and get started. I modestly suggest commencing your journey by reading the following essays and profiles. And, as you'll soon learn, there is too much to experience in a single lifetime. Still, we should give it our best shot. As Etta once said, "You can't anticipate circumstances."

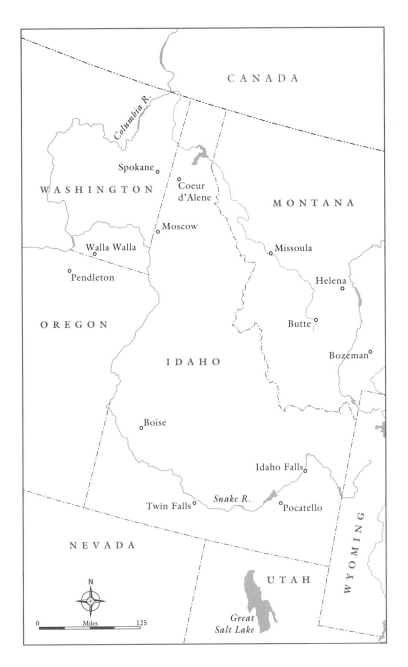

DINING OUT, CAFE STYLE

AT THE CANYON INN, JUST OFF HIGHWAY 12 in Peck, Idaho (population 160), the blackberry pie is served in bowls. Outside, chip trucks and Forest Service rigs shift down along the curvaceous Clearwater River. The cook yells from behind the heat lamps and plate stacks that she will warm up the pie if it's not hot enough. And do I want vanilla ice cream on top? I sit at the counter next to the plywood divider that separates the cafe from the bar. I lean over and look into the bar. The television next to a Confederate flag is on with a *Mash* rerun cabled in from Lewiston, 36 miles to the west. Bottles of beer chill in glass coolers. Aside from the blue glow of the television, Hamm's and Budweiser signs provide the only light in the bar.

Near the cash register are Slim Jim's, Smokey Joes, cartons of cigarettes, trophies, peanuts, plastic lighters, Life-Savers, M&Ms, gum, and dispensers of small aluminum foil packets of Bayer, Anacin, and Tums.

It's Valentine's Day in Idaho, but only a few couples are in the only cafe in Peck. There are no menus. A signboard above the counter lists the day's specials. I have the deluxe cheeseburger with fries for $3.35. Deluxe means pickles, onions, and a stiff wave of iceberg lettuce that contains not a trace of water. Fries are the curly kind and bathed in old grease. I have died and gone to heaven. The cheeseburger is delicious, and I eat it without guilt. I mean, how can you not eat an animal that rears back in fright when confronted with a painted cattle guard?

I exchange weather reports with the waitress, who is also the barmaid and, I think, related to the cook and perhaps part owner. One quick look at me and she knows I'm not from around here. I look too happy, with too much smirk, my hands too soft and clean without enough scars. I'm wearing a $300 leather jacket made from five different types of lamb.

I'm careful not to break any of the handwritten rules hanging on the wall:

CHILDREN ARE FUN TO WATCH. PLEASE WATCH YOURS AND KEEP THEM SEATED.

COFFEE PRICES HAVE GONE UP.

WE ARE NOT THE FIRST NATIONAL BANK. IF WE DON'T KNOW YOU, DON'T ASK TO CASH A CHECK.

DON'T ASK FOR BREAKFAST BETWEEN 11 A.M. AND 4 P.M.

This cafe is the kind of place my grandpa used to take me as a kid. He would flirt with the waitresses and catch up on the local gossip, while I was left alone to gratefully polish off platefuls of artery-clogging burgers washed down with milk shakes spun from real ice cream. Now, whenever I travel, I make it a point to avoid any franchise restaurant and, instead, seek out a local cafe. In this part of the West, cafes are multipurpose facilities, doubling as community centers, meeting halls, and counseling offices. And it's there that you can find the pulse of a town.

One Friday night when my wife and I were in a rush to get somewhere, we stopped at Rose's Cafe in Harrison, Idaho (population 267), where teenage girls wearing their boyfriends' football jerseys filled every available booth and counter seat. The big homecoming game against Clark Fork had just ended, with Harrison coming out on top 26–22. We knew the score because the waitress, who was also the cook, cashier, busperson, and relative to many of the patrons, told us the score before she told us the special: meat loaf sandwiches and potato chips. Outside, pickups cruised Main Street flashing their headlights and honking their horns. Fathers and mothers of the team lined the sidewalk, drinking beers, laughing, and carrying on as if *they* were still in high school.

"We're in kind of a hurry," I said when the waitress finally came over. "What doesn't take long to make?"

"Nothing," she replied. "Do you want coffee while you wait?"

CRANES OVER OTHELLO

HABITAT BIOLOGIST RON FRIESZ climbs up on an idling school bus outside the high school in Othello, Washington, and looks us over. We're a mostly middle-aged group of out-of-towners with water bottles, notepads, and binoculars. It's a brilliant, sunny March morning in the Central Basin, but icy breezes off the nearby Cascades keep us from believing in spring.

Those of us on the bus are not in Othello (population 5,847) to visit the vast, irrigated Russet Burbank potato fields, where the majority of America's french fries begin the journey to our plates. Nor are we here to marvel at the massive U.S. Bureau of Reclamation Central Basin irrigation project that extends from the Grand Coulee Dam 150 miles south to Pasco and turns this desert unnaturally green and makes all those potatoes possible.

We have come to Othello and paid $5.00 each for one reason: to see sandhill cranes.

As the bus lumbers off into the countryside, Friesz, who

has worked for the Washington Department of Fish and Wildlife for twenty-six years, welcomes us to the first annual Sandhill Crane Festival. He tells us the 25,000 cranes that migrate here every year use the surrounding fields and the national refuge as a staging area on their way to their breeding grounds in Alberta, Canada. They have traveled from their winter home in California's Central Valley to Malheur National Wildlife Refuge in central Oregon.

"Nobody knows exactly where they nest in Alberta," Friesz says, creating a wonderful mystery for this busload of birders, many of whom have been coming on their own for years to view the crane migration.

We don't have to travel far to see our first crane. Within a five-minute drive are about one hundred cranes in a cornfield devouring last year's crop, putting on weight for the strenuous work to come during the breeding season. They mate for life, or more than twenty years.

"Now, let's be real quiet as to not disturb them," Friesz whispers, a warning everyone heeds during the three hours we are together, traveling from one flock to the next.

The cranes call softly to each other in a loud purr. In the distance, against a backdrop of fields and basalt cliffs, we can see long rows of cranes in the sky, some circling in a hypnotizing helix to gain altitude. How odd to see such wild, fragile beauty in a landscape dominated and ravaged by agribusiness. How fitting, too. I think of the cranes dropping out of the heavens into Othello as necessary reminders of a larger, more precious world beyond crop yields and french fries. Like all of nature, cranes, if protected, will sustain us in ways that human-made development cannot.

Folks in Othello have discovered that cranes can also be an economic resource. The 400 to 500 birders who came to the festival bought gas and food, and some stayed overnight in local motels. A happy chamber of commerce official could not come up with an official dollar amount, but she did tell me they certainly felt an impact on the town's economy. Plans are already under way for next year's festival.

Many sponsors came together to create this event, including local and state Audubon chapters and employees from the refuge. In addition to the bus tours, the all-day festival included duck identification, mask making, origami, a geology field trip, beginning birding, and a presentation by Thomas Hoffmann, a Seattle board member from the International Crane Foundation based in Baraboo, Wisconsin.

At the presentation, Hoffmann told us that crane fossils have been found alongside dinosaur bones and that the sandhills in Othello are part of three great migratory flocks. The largest group of 500,000, 90 percent of the world's sandhill crane population, migrates to the Platte River in Nebraska, much to the delight of the thousands of birders who come, too. The birding event "Wings over the Platte" is a huge economic boost to small Nebraska towns like Kearney and Grand Island. Those hosting the smaller flocks have a good model to follow.

But not everyone in Othello was welcoming. During one stop, a private property–obsessed landowner came charging up in his pickup, scattering us like quail. He was angry because the school bus was too near his shack, which borders the Columbia National Wildlife Refuge. "Get off of my land," he screamed at the startled bus driver, before launching into a stream of profanities, of which he seemed well versed. We quickly boarded the bus and left him to fume alone in his junk-filled yard. My wife lost her glasses in the rush.

As we drove off, I couldn't resist mouthing the words "We'll be back. Just like the cranes. We'll be back."

WHAT IS A LIFE
WELL LIVED?

"JUST A MINUTE. I HAVE TO PUT MY WIG ON," Etta
yells from somewhere deep inside her wood-frame house.
Well, not exactly yells. Some of her voice and most of her hair
have been taken by ovarian cancer. I'm standing on her porch,
near a century's crop of yellow pines and dusty lilacs, imagining how this view has changed in the eight decades Etta has
called this part of eastern Washington home.

When the door opens, it's not the grim specter of cancer that rushes forward, but, instead, the bright flame of a
rich life. I see that Etta has placed her wig slightly off center;
it dips crookedly in front. She is birdlike, her skin porcelain,
her eyes as blue as a lazuli bunting, and she is shrinking. The
top of Etta's head barely reaches to the level of my chest. We
shake hands, and it's decided—we will become dear friends.

I've come here because I want to meet the artist whose
bird drawings are as evocative and graceful as flight itself.
Except among local birders who covet her interpretations,
Etta's art is a well-kept secret. Only one gallery in town sells

her works, mainly in the form of note cards and small draw-ings. In my living room sits a prized possession—a handmade wooden easel that cradles a scratchboard rendition of a trio of baby barn owls. The drawing fits in the palm of my hand like a playing card. Staring out from tufts of hay, the dark eyes of the owlets follow me as I move around the room. I've come to believe they are trying to give me advice—important advice—urging me to get off the couch (while I still can), put on my boots, grab my binoculars, go outside, and look for them, or for anything flashing at leaf level. What is a life well lived? is what I imagine these owls are asking.

Just beyond Etta's place is the sharp descent to the Snake River canyon. The river is often called "Snake Lake," a sarcastic acknowledgment of slack water shoved back into itself like a boiled cow intestine from the Tri-Cities, Wash-ington, to Lewiston, Idaho. The distance is around 140 miles, one dam every 35 miles.

The four dams are awesome if only for their testament to our Yankee-can-do industriousness and optimism. From 1962, when President Lyndon Johnson switched on the generators at Ice Harbor Dam, until 1975, when the kilo-watts began to register at Lower Granite Dam, we believed anything was possible if enough manpower and cement were employed. Just as in the philosophy of "rain following the plow," we believed that after the completion of the dams, commerce would rush up river, and the region would soon be buzzing with the activity of prosperous cities.

Most of all we proved—again, as if we hadn't known—that we did possess the power to alter nature, to stop a river in its tracks. No matter how shortsighted or destructive, this remains no small feat for a species that once dressed in furs and huddled in caves. The same double-edged, human curiosity is working on a cure for Etta's cancer.

Today, the river's electricity travels south to the boom towns in California and Arizona. The isolated dams sit like misbehaving children sent to their rooms, surrounded by silent, birdless hills of cheat grass, Canada thistle, and wild oats.

Etta's 600-acre spread was a working dryland wheat and pea farm when her husband, former Whitman County commissioner Harry Wegner, was still cancer free and alive. That was more than twenty years ago. Now the home place has settled back into itself, and the neighboring families are increasingly strangers—nonfarmers who work in town.

Etta's farm is in a state of reclamation: Rusted equipment and leaning outbuildings sink into the decay, a tangled orchard needs pruning, and a swimming pool fills with leafy humus and colonies of mice. Someday the land will also swallow Etta, probably while drawing in her studio or watching out the kitchen window for her favorite bird, the California quail.

Inside Etta's house is order: colonial furniture, an upright piano, her own framed artwork, photos of Harry and her two sons, and an immaculate kitchen, where she graciously prepares coffee, dripped Melitta-style, into china tea cups with saucers. We head to the back of the house to her studio, surrounded on three sides by windows that keep watch over a bird kingdom vibrating with quick movements.

Etta asks me to sit down. Like most men and women of her generation, she is embarrassed to talk about herself. *I'm nothing special,* her body language tells me. But I describe for her what the owl drawing means to me, and the note cards that feature chukars, wild turkeys, Hungarian partridge, grouse, pheasants, herons, and a favorite card simply called "Coyote and Canola." I'm gushing with praise, but Etta's thinking about the possibility of a dry winter.

She looks out at her yard and says, "I will miss it if we don't have snow, but no snow will be good for the animals and birds."

I back off, but I still have so many questions. Etta knew the natural history of this area long before the concrete was poured to submerge thousands of acres of habitat. A bridge from the past, she knows how little of that wild world remains. And her tenacious quest over a century to answer simple questions about her surroundings seems an answer to the owlet's question, *What is a life well lived?*

More than a thousand people from Etta's generation die each day in this country. With them goes the knowledge of birds and animals now extinct, the history of farm and soil, the ability to mend fences and keep knives sharp. When the last of this generation passes, who will tell us our stories?

"I've drawn ever since I was in grade school," Etta says. "I would go through periods when I would draw only legs. Then it would be eyes. I must have used up a lot of paper. And I drew all over the margins of my textbooks."

Etta uses pen and ink, scratchboard, watercolor and pastel, and she carefully chooses her papers. Her stippled series of sandhill cranes is printed on sheets of blue marbled paper because "it resembles water clouds." She makes all her own hardwood frames, even the miniature easels: "We're a family of builders."

Tubs of pinecones, abandoned nests, rocks, wings, and feathers crowd her tiny studio, along with dried flowers and "sticks with character." Wings, talons, and a head of a recent hen pheasant roadkill spill across a shelf. "The whole bottom part of my freezer is full of roadkill," she says. Stacks of *National Wildlife* fill her bookshelves, as well as *Nature Conservancy, National Geographic,* and *Washington Wildlife.*

Picture books on nature are everywhere: *Water Prey and Games Birds of North America, The Wonders of Nature,* and *The International Wildlife Encyclopedia.* A loaded camera hangs from a coat rack, and directly outside her studio window stands a birdfeeder she hopes the juncos will discover.

Each day, Etta hikes alone in a small forest she planted long ago of blue spruce, willow, walnut, and honey locust. Quiet miracles occur, even in this transformed agricultural landscape. The miracles, she says, unfold in the curvy "eyebrow places," the old growth hawthorns, and overhead in the thermals with the red-tailed hawks and turkey vultures.

"You can't anticipate circumstances," says Etta, looking up at the sky, planning another sketch, another way of preventing loss.

AWAY FROM THE DAMS AND RESERVOIRS, and the fish ladders that don't work too smoothly, the Snake River narrows and regains its lively figure. Cottonwoods, mullein, and red willow bushes emerge alongside fists of bunch grass. Birds reappear, and not the usual magpie-starling-junco-raven-robin backyard mix we have up on the Palouse Prairie, but grosbeaks, tanagers, warblers, osprey, falcons, wood ducks, cormorants, and grebes. Baskets of oriole nests hang from the trees, and barn owls watch and blink from the basalt rock ledges. From this point, to where 1,421 acres of riparian area are under water up river at Hell's Canyon, Oxbow, and Brownlee dams, the Snake somehow sustains life through its flora and fauna. In that precious stretch of rock and shore you can say the word *river* out loud, and it doesn't feel like a lie.

In the book *River of Life, Channel of Death*, historian Keith Petersen writes, "In 1972 an estimated 22,000 pheasants, 57,000 quail, 20,000 partridges, 52,000 chukars, 120,000 mourning doves, 8,400 cottontails, and 1,800 deer lived within a half mile of the river's edge between Pasco and Lewiston. . . . By 1987, Washington Department of Game officials estimated that the lower Snake supported only 2,000 game birds . . . that the 95,000 wintering songbirds formerly along the river then numbered only 3,000."

In *The Snake River*, Tim Palmer writes of the loss of 14,400 acres of habitat. "The Army Corps estimated losses of 1,800 deer, 120,800 upland game birds and animals, 13,400 fur bearers. . . ."

BUT THESE ARE JUST NUMBERS. Loss of birdsong is almost impossible to record in writing. You need a human voice, preferably an older one.

"When I was small, I built birdhouses and took care of

injured animals," Etta tells me. "I remember on the farm I found an injured pig. I cared for it for three days. Then it died and I cried and cried.

"That's when there were flocks of orioles and mountain bluebirds. Cedar waxwings, too, and the barn swallows in the spring. That locust tree used to be black with barn swallows. The power lines sagged with swallows. Now you are so glad when you see a goldfinch."

She blames the expansion of farming into bird habitats, the draining of wetlands, along with fertilizers, pesticides, and those ever-present dams. "A lot of it is because farmers farm from fence row to fence row," she says. "I've been soap-boxing for forty years about our use of chemicals—the dumping, the throw-away stuff. Rachel Carson's *Silent Spring* had a tremendous effect on me. I became completely organic, hated at that time. I knew I was a pain-in-the-neck for Harry. No one would admit to being 'organic.' It was a bad word, like 'liberal.'"

SALMON ARE THE POSTER CHILDREN of dam-breaching advocates. In the endless yackety-yak of lost farms, extinct fish, and economic models, birds are rarely mentioned. When the floodgates closed and the water bloated hundreds of finger canyons and covered dozens of islands, all that was riparian became a memory, and only for those fortunate enough to have seen the river in its wild state. Soon we forgot about the river altogether as we ran our boats and personal watercraft across that calm surface. The few bones of recreation areas the Army Corps of Engineers threw our way seemed so welcome on those hot August days, when we lay down in cool Kentucky bluegrass under the shade of Russian olive trees—sage and rattlers at a safe distance. Our lives were getting damn complicated, and we deserved to rest next to soothing waters in green parks with flush toilets and full hookups, oases called Chief Timothy, Wawawai, Penawawa, and Boyer.

Despite our best efforts at amnesia, we still hear nagging voices. The river's asleep, some say cautiously. You've been treating her like a woman in bondage. You can't tame her forever. Someday she will wake up, and we will all pay. But it hasn't happened yet, and it probably won't for many generations to come, if ever. There are no guarantees; who knows if the salmon or birds will return if the dams disappear? Yet it's certain that in a few thousand days of political gridlock the argument will be moot.

"A prudent people will not allow the endowments of nature to waste away," President Johnson said that historic day at Ice Harbor Dam. He was a big man, and he loved big ideas. However, the endowment the president referred to was the electrical potential of free-flowing water, not birds or salmon.

I have no relationship or special affinity to salmon. My opinions are mostly politically spoon-fed and lack any anecdotal substance. I've stood at the grimy fish-viewing windows below Lower Granite, but I have seen only bony whitefish and an occasional steelhead. Using the small percentage of my brain that understands scientific processes, a salmon's journey resembles a fairy tale, defying belief in its magic. How could a fish ever travel more than a thousand miles, commence against the raging mouth of the Columbia River, survive hook, net, and turbine, to eventually climb several mountain ranges to tiny Redfish Lake deep in the chambers of Idaho's heart? What triggers such effort?

Birds and animals cannot prepare for political decisions. They can only respond to their instincts and their circumstances. Just east of Etta's farm sits Dworshak Dam, a concrete monster that nearly stops the flow of the Clearwater River's north fork. Each winter dozens of deer, elk, and god-knows-what-other creatures fall through the ice covering the deep water behind Dworshak's face. Hard-wired into the minds of these animals is a migratory passage that no longer leads them over the live river of rocks and reeds but over a deep, unfathomable reservoir of controlled slack water whose bottom is filled with twisted antlers, bleached scapulas, and fractured skulls.

Looking out the window at the only pecan tree in eastern Washington, Etta expresses her sense of loss, her gleaming, hopeful eyes a contradiction. "It's so sad when you think about the creatures that have become extinct: the carrier pigeon, the salmon," she says quietly. "It worries me that so many things are depleting now. Even the raccoons seem to be on the decline. They used to open the door on the back porch."

OVER THE NEXT TWO YEARS I SEE ETTA several more times, and once, she and her son, Alan, come to my house for dinner. After each visit she sends a long letter, written with perfect penmanship, usually with a story like this one about Lolo Pass.

> I couldn't believe what I was seeing—a 3-foot boulder with a perfectly formed bowl (or basin) on top, smooth as if chiseled on a lathe, and nesting in it a little walnut-sized polished rock. Egg shaped. It was so obvious that it had to be the result of rushing water spinning in it for hundreds of years. It was awesome.
>
> That was fifty years ago, and no one knew

about that history. We were a group of eight—
the men decided to climb up the steep mountain,
but I was the only woman, and I struck out in a
different direction so I didn't have anyone with
me to verify what I found. I couldn't take that little rock for proof and break up that companion-
ship after thousands of years. Do rocks have
souls? The Bible says 'Even the stones cry out!'

I tell her of my birding adventures—thousands of
migrating sandhills in central Washington; the American dip-
per unexpectedly found on an Audubon Christmas Bird
Count; a migration of vultures at Idaho's City of Rocks. She,
in turn, hands me her latest project—sketches of herons, so
perfect as if to suggest she once lived among them.

Our last visit is in early spring; the wheat is just greening
up, and crop dusters roar overhead and spill their chemicals
across the hills. I'm moving to Illinois, where I will have to
learn an entirely new batch of birds, along with rivers and
trees. I don't even suggest that Etta come visit the Land of
Lincoln. Besides, she isn't going anywhere. There remains so
much to learn on her small patch of earth, delicious questions that only art and birds will answer.

Against the greatest of odds, she has defeated one of the deadliest forms of cancer. Her hair has returned, white and thick. All those trips alone for chemo in Pullman paid off. About the chance of reoccurrence she says, "I don't worry about it. I've lived more than my share of years." Soon she will turn ninety. All gravy from here on out.

She puts her hand—the same one that still moves so steadily across sketchpads, the fingers that so long ago repaired injured animals—on my waist for one last photograph. Her head tilts and tucks under my shoulder like a grebe in repose. Who would ever want to let go?

Am I dreaming, or are there more birds this year than last? A flock of white-crowned sparrows work the shrubs near my house, and a lone black-capped chickadee divides his song into a two-part cadence. Down in the canyon, deep within tepid waters, salmon pick their way through the fish ladders and, like Etta, cling to life, to beauty, to unanticipated circumstances. Seen in the right light, through Etta's eyes, for instance, all of it is a miraculous gift.

LOOKING FOR
MR. GOODBUG

I HAVE AN ENTOMOLOGIST FRIEND who disputes my claim that certain insects have brains. My theory took root around the time of my first sighting of a praying mantis, whose large triangular frontal lobe, compound eyes, and slow, methodical head movements convinced me that this was a bug with big ideas.

My friend laughed when I laid out my anecdotal supposition. "No," he said, "like all insects, praying mantises are as dumb as onions." I wanted to counter by saying that if onions were so stupid, how come they make us cry? But I kept quiet, for once. Besides, he is a respected scientist, and I slinked out of college freshman biology the day we were ordered to pith frogs.

The entomologist continued by saying that praying mantises, members of the *Mantidae* family, are in the United States by accident. They are also so cannibalistic that they are inefficient predators, even of caterpillars. That's why you rarely see more than one mantis at a time. Just how smart is it to eat your own species?

One August night, in a one-room cabin in western Montana, a half-filled (or was it half-empty?) glass of water became a final resting place for a host of drowned insects. Tiny green flyers, mosquitoes, lacewings, and even a suicidal moth, whose chalky body turned the water the color of steel, floated on top. During my weeklong stay, I never emptied the glass, and each morning brought a new layer of entomological corpses, most of which I could not identify.

In Montana, insects intruded on my thoughts and tested my philosophy of not killing them on sight. (I allow some wriggle room for spiders large enough to make floorboards creak.) Bugs cannot be ignored. *Notice me!* the swarm of gnats insists, moving like smoke down the path along the lake. *Beware my bite!* warn the aggressive yellow jackets at dinner who, despite the entomologist's opinion, seem to possess the mental capacity to cop a bad attitude. Spiders trek up the cabin's walls, startling me with their silent stalking. When they got too close, I swept them into a yogurt container and flung them outside, peeking back into the container before carrying it inside, just to make sure.

In seventh grade, at DeWitt Clinton Grade School in Chicago, we were shown a film of a scientist unearthing 1 square foot of black, Illinois topsoil. The scientist, wearing a white lab coat, placed the block of dark dirt on a stainless steel table and proceeded to pick it apart with a metal pointer. Hundreds of varieties of beetles, worms, centipedes, ants, silverfish, and hard-shelled ribbed insects (some of which I recognized from my childhood apartment) scrambled for cover, seeking the damp humus shelter from which they had been uprooted. This display was astonishing to a city kid. In just a few minutes I learned that soil teemed with secret life. I realized for the first time that I needed to tread lightly, look closely, and, most importantly, take nothing for granted.

Recent calculations of the actual number of living species of all organisms on Earth place the figure at approximately 1.4 million. Of that frequently disputed amount, 750,000 are insects, and of that number, 9,000 are known species of ants. Myrmecologists suspect the actual number might be three times higher. E. O. Wilson writes that, unlike humans, an ant knows what it will do each day of its short life. The oldest ants in a colony are sent out to do the most dangerous work, keeping the younger ants safely near the domain of the queen. Ants move ten times their weight and can withstand huge doses of radiation. They are regimented, disciplined, and can survive huge population losses. Harvester ants once even frustrated waste disposal methods at the Idaho National Engineering Laboratory by moving buried low-level radioactive soil to the surface. It's obvious that ants, along with cockroaches, plastics, and coyotes, will long outlive our more evolved species of frontal lobed contemplators and schemers.

But for reproductive practicality, you can't beat the Sierra dome spider, which also resides at Flathead Lake. Researcher Paul Wilson writes in *Natural History* magazine that within a 150-foot radius around his cabin there are perhaps three hundred female Sierra dome spiders. Among this spider's many talents is the female's remarkable ability to control conception during mating. Watson writes, "Although more work is needed to be certain, dissections suggest that a female 'chooses' which male sires her brood by opening or closing off her sperm-receiving ducts, thereby controlling fertilization of the eggs. . . . Females have evolved the equipment to dominate the ultimate decision as to which males will sire the spiderlings. . . ." Now, this is a contraceptive method women might wholeheartedly embrace.

ON THE SUNDAY BEFORE I LEFT MY HOME in eastern Washington to come to Montana, I noticed that each sticky leaf on my backyard maple was covered with ladybugs, which were helping themselves to generous portions of aphids. I remembered that lady beetles breed exclusively on plants and trees that contain their main food supply—aphids. Are these actions of low intelligence?

I wonder if my entomologist friend has correctly identified intelligence, associating it only with books, medicine, abstract art, the Internet, and regular reading of the *Times*. Because he is a scientist, I hope he might consider the conclusion I had reached, one that began in seventh grade: that we know very little about what actually goes on above our heads, underneath our feet, and in the dusty corners of the rooms we sleep in at night. And isn't that admission comforting, knowing how the natural world is carefully scrutinizing us?

TEACHING THE WAY
OF THE WOLF

KEITH MARSHALL, PACK CARETAKER at the Wolf Education and Research Center in Winchester, Idaho, tells me to squat in the wet snow and, in a show of respect to wolves, press my palm to the fence.

"Do not be afraid," I tell myself. "Remember, you grew up on the South Side of Chicago."

Out of the woods trot all eleven members of the Sawtooth Pack. By this time, Keith is within the twenty-acre enclosure. I am not invited inside, which is just fine. The wolves do not know my voice, my scent, or my gait. Besides, I am intimidated—no, *scared* is a more honest description—of such close proximity to wildness. Instead I am told to keep quiet and not to make any sudden movements. Trembling is OK.

Marshall first greets the alpha male Kamots ("To Go Free"), who, in a show of superiority, holds his tail higher than the rest of the pack. Initially, Marshall pays the most attention to Kamots to reaffirm to the pack that he accepts their choice as leader. Kamots is a strong but just leader, Marshall says, who is not afraid to dance and jump with the other members of the pack. "I admire him personally," he says. "If more leaders were like him, we'd have fewer problems."

The other wolves are glad to see Marshall, too, who has been out of town the last four days at a conference. A couple of the younger wolves stand on their hind legs and place their front paws on his shoulders. Keith gently puts these wolves down on their sides and rolls them over in a subtle show of dominance—his own form of pack etiquette.

As Marshall wrestles another wolf down, he talks about his full-time responsibilities as caretaker of the wolves and the surrounding 300 acres the WERC leases from Idaho's Nez Perce tribe: "You just don't deal with one wolf. You deal with the whole pack. We respect the wolves' space at all times."

Kamots notices my palm and walks over, sniffs it, then licks it through the chain link. One by one the remaining ten members of the pack repeat Kamots's behavior. Then all hell breaks out. Pack behavior: Bared teeth and snarky snaps. Wide, wild, yellow eyes. Quick, deft movements in the snow, reminding me of dance. I slowly take my hand from the fence and listen to my heart pounding a path out of my body.

Nothing in this fighting suggests domesticity. These are not dogs. Kamots disciplines unruly pack members Wahoots ("Howls a Lot") and his sister Weyekin ("Spirit Guide") by grabbing their muzzles in his mouth. Other wolves also aggressively charge and pounce, until the pecking order is back in place and it is clear who is boss. It is neither Keith nor me.

The ruckus ends abruptly, and several of the wolves sit down in the snow and begin to howl. This is not a "nature sounds" CD. Real live howling fills the woods, silencing the nearby ravens, and just for a moment I can imagine another era when wild animals outnumbered the likes of us. How did we get so unconnected from wolves and their habitat? Here in Winchester there are answers.

"I interact with them daily," says Marshall, who has lived with the wolves for a year and a half and has finely tuned all his senses to the natural rhythms of bird, weather, and, most of all, wolf. "They provide me with the opportunity to better understand people. Since they are in a social unit, there's a lot of behavior that is similar to the way people respond to each other.

"But they are not spiteful like humans. Fur color doesn't matter either. They also point out the subtleties and rhythms of nature. Ten years after I leave this place I'll still be dissecting what I've learned."

Megan Parker, a research biologist at the center, has lived with the wolves for four years and has done vocalization research with the pack, along with hierarchy behavior, monitoring, and habitat work. She echoes Marshall's admiration.

"Wolves are an incredible resource here," she says. "Being with them is such a privilege. They have taught me how to pay attention. I'm more prepared for even human behaviors and how to respond to a pack dynamic."

Marshall's job is to pass on that learning potential to visitors, who are usually not allowed to touch the fence. The number of visitors is also carefully monitored so as to not disturb the pack.

"We're about being subtle," he says. "When you come here, be prepared to view the world in a new way through the eyes of a wolf. Be prepared to see the eagle, the mole, the grasshopper, the raven in ways you've never seen before.

"You'll see nature. You'll see everything in a new light. You'll learn empathy, not just for the wolf but for all of nature."

THE PACK, RAISED IN CAPTIVITY by filmmaker Jim Dutcher and his caretakers, and brought to Winchester in 1996, are featured in his films *Wolf: Return of a Legend* and *Wolves at*

Our Door. The wolves provide a living, breathing example for the 13,000-member organization based in Boise whose mission is to "provide public information and scientific research concerning the gray wolf and other endangered species integral to wolf habitat in the Northern Rockies."

Tubal ligation prevents the Sawtooth females from having pups. None of these wolves will ever return to the Idaho wilds.

Wolves are a tough sell in Idaho, especially among non-Indians, who have inherited the mythology of the "big, bad wolf" from their European ancestors. When Marshall addressed an RV club one summer at Winchester State Park, he got an earful of mostly negative, but not atypical, opinions: "Humans have dominion over nature"; "It's those damn Easterners who want to save them"; "Our tax dollars used to go to killing them, now our taxes are going to save them!"

Marshall probably didn't change that audience's opinion, but he says he softened them: "If they can't like wolves, maybe they can like me. It's a start."

Marshall, other WERC staff, and members of the Nez Perce tribe also visit schools in an attempt to shatter the age-old myths of the big, bad wolf among a younger generation that is more open to new ways of viewing the natural world. One program, "Wolf Box," reaches 30,000 schoolchildren in Idaho and Montana annually. Put together by the National Wildlife Federation and the U.S. Forest Service, this traveling educational kit includes a video, puppets, books, wolf pelts, plaster-cast wolf tracks and actual skulls, and other classroom aids.

Levi Holt, a Nez Perce tribal member and the area manager for the center, grew up with a different mythology of wolves. He says Native Americans and wolves share similar histories. Both were persecuted and forced into smaller and smaller habitats, and both used their "cunning to move away from the two-leggeds to the far north and mountains." Because of that shared experience Holt says, Native Americans feel a special affinity with wolves. Today the Nez Perce have the main lead and responsibility for wolf recovery in Idaho. At the time of this writing, an estimated 300 wolves lived in Idaho's wilds.

"Since time immemorial the Nez Perce have watched, observed, and learned from the animal world," Holt says. "The wolves represent to me a reconnection of a lost spirit. The wolf is one of the missing links in the Sacred Circle. It gives all Indian people a newfound energy."

Holt's great grandparents gave him the name Black Beaver when he was a child, and recently he understood why.

"The beaver is a builder using Mother Earth's timber and hair," Holt said. "It was finally revealed to me that I would work with wood in the same way."

Holt designed and helped build the Interpretive Center for the Wolf Education and Research Center in Winchester, Idaho. The structure is built in the whole earth tradition of a Nez Perce longhouse, with natural materials of earth and straw, clay and mud and concrete.

Holt is also a student of the wolves. "One thing that has come into my heart is that in many ways wolves have a healing power," he says. Holt tells a story to prove his point.

One summer a girl suffering from a fatal nervous disorder contacted Wishing Star Foundation to request her final days be spent in the company of the Idaho wolves. For five days and nights she lay sick in a yurt next to the Sawtooth Pack enclosure. From her bed she could hear the wolves howl.

"The wolves seemed to sense her illness," Holt said, suggesting that it was a pack decision.

After the five days her health improved, and her mother remarked to Holt, "She displays and shows a different kind of strength than I've ever seen before."

The girl is still alive. She plans to return to Winchester, to revisit the pack.

Not far from where the girl stayed is an interpretive sign with a quote from Chief Dan George:

"If you talk to the animals, they will talk with you, and you will know each other. If you do not talk to them, you will not know them, and what you do not know you will fear. What one fears, one destroys."

COMMUTING WITH
DAUGHTER

FOUR O'CLOCK AND I ARRIVE to pick up my daughter, Rose, in front of the Moscow, Idaho, Public Library. She sits on the west-facing stone stairs, the unused entrance to the old Carnegie section that now houses children's books. On the stairs with Rose is Rachel, also of the Moscow High School ("Pride of the North") class of 1998. Here sit two seventeen-year-olds deep in conversation and school about to end for the year. The weak rays of this spring's on-and-off sun hit their faces and hair in such a way as to warm the coldest heart with youth and promise.

This is May on the Palouse, a tender time when the fat buds of ancient lilac bushes break apart and seduce us with scent. From every distant corner of town cock pheasants call in their hens, and quail offer their high purrs. Finches, mourning doves, and black-capped chickadees compete for birdsong space and nesting sites. Cottonwood flotsam drifts overhead like snow. I feel lazy, almost drowsy, so I sit in the car and drink it all in for a moment, letting the nonsense of the electronic workday evaporate, and hoping the girls don't spot me.

I've been picking Rose up after school for years at the library. Most afternoons I find her curled up with a book or magazine in the back room; lately, in these teenage years, she sits close to her boyfriend, John, at a secluded table, sometimes studying and sometimes pretending to study. She is rarely late, always dependable except for once.

Two years ago, on a brilliant Indian summer day, she and John, in the midst of stealing time together, walked out of school after third period to take turns calling in sick from a phone booth, lowering their voices in their best parental imitations, which were as transparent as cellophane to the school secretary.

John's father called me at work with one of those "We have a problem" messages, which means "I have a problem that involves you, and now we have a problem that I expect you to help me solve." John had finally turned up at home and come clean with the whole scam. I found Rose exactly where I knew she would be: at the library, calmly reading. What followed could be classified as an authentic "scene"— a scolding in my fiercest father voice, Rose defiantly denying, then giving in to confession and tears. She said they'd only been drinking coffee at Third Street Market (for four hours!), and, besides, school was boring. I sat in front of her, brought those tears right out, and gave her an earful about responsibility and truth, then questioned her sudden interest in coffee. (I never mentioned, of course, that I walked out of high school in Chicago my junior year to protest the shootings at Kent State, but instead of going to an antiwar rally, I spent the afternoon in the left field bleachers of Wrigley Field watching the Cubs lose.)

Nearby, in the library, a young mother carrying her baby in a trendy Mayan wrapping glared at me with disapproval. "Just you wait," I thought. "That cute cherub baby sucking on fruit leather will someday carve deep worry wrinkles into your healthy face. It won't even matter if you are a vegetarian, a New Ager, or a lifelong member of the Green Party. There may come a point when you question if in fact this is your child, instead suspecting that she is the product of an egg dumper, a human cowbird. And someday you may even regret not eating your young."

The next morning I had the vice principal, Mr. Whitmore, a large, somber man with the strut of a small-town cop, who has seen them all and heard every excuse, haul Rose out of third-year Spanish into his office, where I sat waiting (surprise!). The vice principal frightened me, bringing back the terror of the Chicago public school system where I labored for twelve years with more than one trip to a vice principal for an attitude adjustment. For this visit, I had ironed my best Gap pants and a conservative white shirt, and put on my least scuffed shoes. I matched up my socks, dug out a tie, and attempted a dimpled Windsor knot. I wanted Mr. Whitmore to see that he was not dealing with trailer trash from the Idaho bomb belt; that we owned bookcases that actually held books, not rifle parts and piles of *TV Guide;* that I did not fear my government; and that even though Rose was failing geometry, this cutting of school was simply an aberration, a slight bump on an otherwise smooth road toward middle-class adulthood. While more tears squeezed down her cheeks, she got a tough-love lecture from an authority figure other than me, a Saturday of detention (with John, unfortunately), and a barrel of public shame. After she left, with a look toward my direction not unlike the one I received from the young mother at the library, the vice principal turned to me and said, "You know, I'm glad you did that. Most of the parents here try to cover up for their kids. No one takes responsibility anymore. In fact, most parents would not have come in at all."

It was all I could do to smile a thank you in his direction. What I really wanted to do was rush after Rose, apologize for causing her any discomfort, then buy her a mint chip ice-cream cone. (Please don't hate me!) I felt awful for embarrassing her, like I was headed for an appearance on the *Montel Williams* show—"Mean fathers who go too far and the daughters who hate them"—but she hasn't cut school since, and she passed geometry.

I LOOK AWAY FROM THE GIRLS across the street to a long staircase leading to the Russell Elementary School playground, where, on a fall day ten years ago, I watched Rose climb those two dozen stairs alone and, with a bag lunch, a cigar box full of colored pens, a gum eraser, and blunt scissors, begin her slow ascent out of my life into first grade.

I ALWAYS LOOK FORWARD TO THIS after-school hour with Rose. It's an important father-daughter time for us, these twenty-five minutes in the car west over the Idaho–Washington border to Pullman, where we've lived since I remarried. A 1989 Subaru hatchback may be an unlikely setting in which to communicate ethics and values, and reaffirm love and family, but it works for us. Anyway, as a parent of a teenager, you are always off balance, grasping at straws, parenting books, or a bottle of Zoloft. So you tend to stay with any small success. Sociologists love to rattle off statistics about how many minutes per day fathers spend talking with their children, always discounting the power of silent communication and the value of mere presence, along with the all-important fatherly stare and raised eyebrows. And they rarely speak of how little or erratically a teenager wants to relate with any parent.

Commutes have definite advantages. A moving car does not allow for any getaways; there is only the window to stare out of, although I'm sure we've both felt like flipping the handle, screaming, and jumping out. We know each other so well that we can slash and hurt in the time it takes to tie a shoe. We've taken turns apologizing, yelling, and, in our worse moments, picking at old scabs to get the blood flowing. ("I didn't ask to live in two homes!" is her worst.) But we also discuss our own modest history, the state of affairs with her friends, and sometimes her mom. I let her speak first, and failing that, I ask some questions not so cleverly disguised to elicit more than a yes or no, or a nod, which is hard to see when you are driving 55 miles an hour on a two-lane highway. "What did you have for lunch? Did you eat lunch? Where? Do you have any homework?" If it's a good day, a "thumbs-up day," as her first grade PE teacher called it, she has a lot to say. "I got two poems accepted in the literary magazine, and I think I'm getting an A in chemistry." But if the day turned sour, and they often do, she gets into the car lugging a stone wall to place between us.

If she is noticeably quiet, I wait it out, knowing that by the time we cross the state line, she might offer something about her lousy day. It might be a friend that she's upset with, or a teacher who lost her extra credit project, or a substitute teacher ridiculed her in front of the class about her negative feelings concerning the Vietnam War, or a word in a poem that was changed without her permission. When she lost a homework file to a temperamental school computer, she asked, "Why do we have to be so dependent on these computers?" by which time she's bent over, crying into her hair.

This little intersection of the library and school at Jefferson and First streets is in many ways the core of our fourteen-year history in this town. And although there has been no change in the surroundings of this corner, Rose is now a young woman of seventeen, and somehow I've managed to turn middle-aged, my face a map of well-earned worry wrinkles.

There's comfort with the same surroundings and disruption with too many changes. Lately, as I look around our home territory beyond this corner, it's disruption that has the upper hand. Here's what's been happening:

Bowlerama, Moscow, Idaho's only independently owned bowling alley, was torn down to make room for a new Wendy's. Down the street, Hardee's opened a year ago, but it just closed. It was remodeled as a Jack-in-the-Box, where Rose and Rachel now work. Arby's opened its second store, on the south part of town as part of a new Chevron mini-mart, directly across the street from 7-11. The new Chevron has more than thirty gas pumps. Burger King, Pizza Hut (Moscow's second), and Taco Bell recently teamed up to create a "food court" on the main floor of the University of Idaho Student Union Building. McDonald's opened a second store in Moscow on the east side, not far from Tidyman's, which replaced a wheat and pea field. The newer McDonald's is smaller, without a kid's fun room. Across the street from Tidyman's, at the Eastside Market-place (actually a mall), rumors have it that Hasting's, a book and entertainment store, may take over the slot left empty when Sears closed. Kentucky Fried Chicken just broke ground. Wal-Mart has been in operation for several years now, and near its location—on Warbonnet Avenue—a sign says Moscow will have a new Staples office supply store by the fall. Ernst closed this year, but there are rumors of an Eagle landing in the same spot. Waremart, a bulk grocery store, remodeled the old K-Mart at the Palouse Empire Mall and opened last fall. The Moscow–Pullman highway past the mall to the Washington state line was widened last year from two lanes to five lanes.

In Pullman, Shop-Ko built a giant store on Grand Avenue and gave away hot dogs on its opening day. Everyone says this will finish off PayLess, which is just a block away. Starbucks opened within the past year just at the eastern entrance to the Washington State University campus, about a half mile from downtown. Starbucks has also taken over the coffee concession on both campuses. This may have led to the closure of the Combine, a downtown coffee and deli fixture that featured live music for more than a decade. An alternative may be the new Denny's, which is not far from the new Holiday Inn Express and the site of a future Inn America. Finch's Groceries and Meats, family-owned for half a century and at its present location for thirty years, closed this spring, but Videoland kicked off the opening of its new stores (one in Moscow and one in Pullman) with giant search lights in both towns that circled the sky for several nights.

In addition, we have seen the boom of cul-de-sacs and housing developments with names like Quail Run, Cottage Estates, and Rolling Meadows. We have more cars and a more impatient class of drivers not afraid to lift the middle finger or tailgate and lean on the horn. More trash from the new fast-food joints. More baseball caps turned backwards. More sameness.

And so it was a year ago on a Friday night that I stood at another Moscow intersection, Third and Main, and for a long, disorienting moment I could not recognize where I was. Traffic roared by without relief—brand-new $35,000 club cab pickup trucks that will never see a flake of hay in their beds. Gangsta rap poured from cars at assault decibels. Red ambulance lights flashed across the street, and paramedics attended to a diabetic who was drunk, like a scene out of the television show *Cops*. I recognized no one in the throng of passersby. People seemed intent on arriving someplace fast, but I didn't know where and was sure I was not invited. They seemed overdressed for northern Idaho. The air smelled like a mix of perfume and car exhaust. Many negative thoughts and unpleasant phrases came to mind. "We're all just monkeys with car keys," was one. Then I thought I was having a stroke.

I wonder if Rose and her generation feel as much grief as I do with these changes. I can't assume they do, although they have plenty of anxious feelings. It's a common mistake to think our kids are carbon copies of us, that through some kind of experiential osmosis their lives mirror ours. But Rose is part of a new generation of westerners who have, in fact, only lived here while many of us grew up elsewhere. They may have no sense of grief about a wheat field turning into a Wal-Mart. Or a clear-cut in the wilderness. Or a new trailer park on the edge of town that replaced an aspen grove. Do we appear angry and sad to our children when they listen to us discuss environmental and social issues? Are we supposed to teach them that grief? Have we already?

I think back to an assignment I gave Spokane high school students when I was invited there as a guest writer, "What Are You Afraid Of?"

Making a mistake. Rapists. Going to college. Becoming my father. Staying the same too long. Environment becoming bad. The future. Death of a loved one. Admitting my love for another. Spiders. My grandmother's perfume. Losing my convictions. Loneliness. Leaving behind what I love. Prejudice. Being torn from all I believe in. Not being able to make a difference. Machines. Dark basements. Raising my children wrong.

We should memorize this list.

❧ ❧

I KNOW SOME THINGS ABOUT MY DAUGHTER. My life is defined by being her father. Rose affects me at both a cellular and an emotional level, in ways so subtle, deep, and even biological that I cannot imagine ever living in a world in which she did not exist. She is always on my mind, sometimes out front, sometimes at the edges, but always there. (Thus the worry wrinkles and crow's-feet.) Yet I cannot always remember her early years with much detail. We did not keep a baby book. There are no videos, thank goodness. Relatives were all back in the Midwest or the East, not a part of my life then. Photos were few, and now they are scattered between two households. I mostly remember being tired and frustrated, trying to climb out of poverty and sort out why I wasn't becoming middle class like everyone else in my generation. For several years I made $130 a week, and each time my boss would hand me the check, he would hold the other end for just a second too long and ask, "Do you mind waiting a day before you cash this?" Despite my erratic memory, there are times, seasonal and aromatic in nature, involving light or sounds or colors, when I do remember details. The way she felt on my back as I carried her down the street. How she would point and crow when I would tell her words to give her vocabulary. The way she would greet me when I returned at the end of the day, exhausted from picking daffodils, driving grain trucks, or cooking omelets.

Rose is leaving, not permanently, but certainly she's ascending another flight of stairs to a new level of life, and this time the lump in my throat is the size of a pineapple. The question is not whether she is prepared but whether I am.

I never imagined how fast we would arrive at this crossroads. Rose is at that magical age, on the doorstep of possibility, about to enter a rarefied state of young adulthood, where excitement and enchantment collide and the world is vast and beckoning. I am mostly settled, feeling those enhanced emotional moments of inspiration less and less, but instead experiencing a richness that I never felt at seventeen, a context and texture that come with being alive for four decades. Some goals remain. I still hope to walk the Pacific Crest Trail, or visit Tuscany, or learn to play tenor saxophone, get a degree in natural science, play guitar like Chet Atkins, and get published in the *New Yorker.*

✒ ✒

ON FATHER'S DAY I DECIDE we should drive to Elk River, a sleepy timber town on life support. Not long ago, customers at the Elk Butte Log Inn watched a logging truck rumble by every three minutes. Those days are mostly over—in the immediate area, at least. The population sign says 149. Another sign in an abandoned building reads COMING SOON, but no one believes it. The only school finally closed several years ago, after graduating its last two high school students, and has been replaced with a few gift shops. Just outside town we are delayed by hundreds of cattle sauntering down the middle of the highway. At the end of the herd is a family on foot using sticks and tree limbs to keep the cattle on track.

Some arm twisting was involved to get Rose to agree to this trip. "Can't I just take you out for breakfast?" she asks, looking pained. We negotiate. I tell her we don't have to leave until eleven, and I agree to buy her a steamed milk on the way.

We rent a canoe at Huckleberry Heaven and put in near the Elk River pond. First we have to negotiate a narrow channel. We have canoed together only one other time, and it's a struggle to synchronize our J strokes. We crash into a few bushes along the bank, get stuck on every sandbar, and manage to cover a hundred yards going sideways. Neither of us gets mad, and the idea of Rose being in a canoe under paternal duress passes with each paddle. Besides, we are out on the water with the turtles, a family of Canada geese, ducks, and a watchful pair of osprey. I don't ever want the day to end.

As we eat cold pasta salad and rhubarb muffins in silence (while high-centered on a sandbar), I wonder what Rose is afraid of, but I don't ask. She has enough to think about. Instead I say, "There's some potato salad and grapes if you're still hungry." I think I'm finally beginning to get it: Rose is mostly grown up. I need to step back even more and let her grow into her life. And I need to get on with mine.

After two hours of canoeing, of which the last part is spent floating in circles around a smaller pond full of warm algae that I tell Rose is actually body snatcher people, we pull the canoe out on the bank and head back. "Let's take the long way, the dirt road to Helmer. We haven't been on it in a few years," I suggest, wanting to draw the afternoon out into twilight and to go somewhere that hasn't been subdivided. But even out here there is change.

After just a mile of driving comes evidence of every conceivable type of logging practice: clear-cuts, selected cuts, burns, and new plantings. New roads are everywhere, with numbered signs, and many have the ubiquitous locked green gates. Rusty culverts lie in piles like intestines, along with discarded steel cables, parked bulldozers, and other earth movers. I look for a campground that I'm convinced is out here, but I can't find it among all the chaos. Signs warn us to watch for heavy equipment, but it's Sunday, and even the work of destruction needs to rest.

I start in with my usual rant and rave about all the new roads, the wreck and ruin, the shrinking habitat for animals, overpopulation, and de-evolution, but after a few minutes I shut up. I can tell where this is going. What do I expect Rose to do? Come out here and blockade a bulldozer? Spike a tree? She's heard all this before. She'll figure it out for herself, if she hasn't already. Or maybe she won't. These are my struggles. She has the rest of her life to acquire her own. Besides, what the loggers—what we—have left is stunning: dark cedar forests and wide, wet meadows of tall grass, skunk cabbage, and wildflowers; creeks that make you weep with their simplicity.

"Aren't the meadows beautiful, Rose? Is that foxglove? And look, larkspur already, and yellow peas, lupine, and red-shafted flickers. And look at all the new trees coming up in that burned-out area. Amazing. Maybe we'll see a cougar or a badger. Remember when you saw your first moose? Isn't summer just the best time? Isn't it glorious?"

WHY I RIDE
THE BUS

ONLY ONE OTHER PASSENGER WAITS to catch the 6:47 A.M. commuter bus from Pullman to Moscow, Idaho. She is pleasant looking, well dressed, with Walkman headphones snaking up out of her sweater. Because I ride this bus regularly, I've learned some details of this woman's life. Whitney Houston is her favorite singer. Her preferred seat on the bus is the one directly behind the driver. I guess her age at thirty, although she acts much younger. She works at Wal-Mart, and, at any moment, she may break out in song or talk to herself in a loud voice. She is not like the rest of us.

The rest of us are a quiet bunch who commute the 8 miles to work or school. Through generous subsidies, Wheatland Express provides free bus service for faculty, staff, and students at the University of Idaho and Washington State University.

Because of this bus service, more than 450 vehicles are kept off the narrow, two-lane Moscow–Pullman road every day. I chose public transportation to drive less and save energy and to make a small contribution to preserving precious resources. But my tiny gift to energy conservation likely makes no difference in our warming planet.

My real reason for commuting is the woman who sings along with Whitney Houston. She is so delightfully different from the people I will work and converse with the rest of the day. From the controlled environment of my office I will talk about publication deadlines and photo placement, and discuss at length the excruciating minutiae of the English language. I will also gossip with coworkers and jockey for professional advancement. But I will not approach anything like the simple honesty of the woman on the bus. She is herself. Most of the time I am role playing.

For fifteen minutes those of us sharing the morning will accommodate this special woman. If she demands that one of us vacate her favorite seat, we do it. If she asks a question, we answer it, even if the question is in the form of word salad. No raised eyebrows, no suggestive sighs, and no smirks.

"Hello, Wal-Mart!" the woman who is not like us yells joyously, as we approach the big store. In unison we all look toward Wal-Mart. A giant American flag flies straight out, pointing east. Behind the store a hawk, a northern harrier, follows the contours of a landscape that resembles the dimples of a golf ball. Deer browse in the tall, mature wheat. Sun pours over the hills, and a line of cars, vans, and trucks heads east and west—all with lone drivers listening to Bob Edwards, Dr. Laura, Jim Rome, and Don Imus.

As he does every morning, the bus driver passes the scheduled stop at the Palouse Empire Mall and, instead, drives a few hundred feet closer to the Wal-Mart parking lot.

No one complains about the special treatment. The woman departs, and the bus driver waits to make sure she's pointed in the right direction. She walks off toward work, where she will tie a blue apron around her waist and begin her shift.

Five months later, on a blustery, wind-chill Friday evening just before Christmas, we stop at the mall for a man who has a shopping cart filled with bags of groceries from WinCo. Four inches of fresh snow have stranded the cart, and the man tries desperately to push it to the bus stop. But the bus pulls ahead to the man, who takes three trips to load his groceries onto two seats. I ask him if he needs a hand, but he refuses in broken English.

He's part of a large contingent of foreign students at the universities who depend on public transportation. For some, owning a vehicle is an unattainable luxury.

After he's settled, surrounded by white plastic bags—twelve in all—the bus pulls onto the highway toward Pullman, and the driver turns off the interior lights.

This is one of my favorite moments. In the dark, with the heater running, I feel safe, surrounded by these strangers, sharing a common experience.

As we arrive on the outskirts of Pullman, I wonder how the man will carry all those food bags to his home. I decide that I will help him. But at the Stadium Way stop, his wife is waiting for him. She is dressed in clothes that are from a country far away, maybe Latvia or Armenia. He again makes three trips back and forth with the groceries, piling them on the curb. They stand opposite each other, a two weeks' supply of food between them.

Then he does something as universal and ancient as snow. He smiles and touches her cheek in a greeting as tender and loving as I've ever witnessed between two people.

This is why I ride the bus. I would never see these dynamic, one-of-a-kind acts of public affection from my private car. Nor would I have the opportunity—the privilege, really—to interact with strangers and to test the limits of my tolerance and generosity. I never expected to find such defining moments before my first cup of coffee.

All around us rush-hour traffic catapults by, and some cars honk and race their engines. I can't imagine why they are in such a hurry.

FEAR OF FLYING, WESTERN STYLE

WE WILL KNOW WHEN OUR LIVES have truly changed in these times of terror threats when the small aircraft—affectionately called "puddle jumpers" by locals—that putter around the inland West actually install cabin doors instead of the standard-issue curtains. But hijackers have never been the real threat on these planes. No, it's the flight itself.

Not too long ago, I boarded a Metro III, a two-prop airplane operated by Big Sky Airlines in Spokane, Washington, for a two-hour trip to Billings, Montana, with one stop in Great Falls. The plane held about sixteen passengers in two single rows. The cabin ceiling was so low that I had to imitate Groucho Marx as I found my seat. My spirits fell immediately when I saw there was no bathroom . . . and no steward. I knew from past experiences that in exactly thirty minutes I would have to use a bathroom. And who would go over the safety features?

The infamous curtain separated us from the lone pilot, who never closed the curtain except to turn around and ask if we were hot. No one answered, probably because we were all coming to the same realization: We had made a big mistake.

Flying in tiny planes is how you get around in the West. I'm quite experienced in this mode of travel, but I like it less with each passing flight, whether my destination is Boise or Moses Lake. Each trip on Horizon, Alaska, or Big Sky has always felt like another precious flake of luck expended.

As we climb to cruising altitude—a mere 15,000 feet— and I hear the clanging of what I think are pieces of the fuselage peeling away, I try to calm my nerves and my singing bladder with a short story by Richard Ford titled "Jealous."

A boy who lives with his father in Dutton, Montana, is being driven to a train station in Shelby by his aunt. Soon they find themselves negotiating a blizzard. Aunt Doris remarks, "I really don't like Montana. And I particularly hate the roads. There's only one way to get anywhere. It's better seen from an airplane."

From this tiny aircraft I can look north at the great Idaho lakes—Coeur d'Alene, Pend Oreille, Priest—and all the rivers and ponds that lead up the steep watersheds of the Bitterroot Mountains to the Montana border. I also think I can spot loose rivets on the plane's wing. The turbulence is breathtaking. My stomach whirls.

The one pilot, Rusty, is just a few feet in front of me. I can almost touch him from my seat. I can see everything he is doing. I wish I couldn't. He looks like he is wrestling a rabid wolverine. It looks like Rusty is losing.

We cross into the Big Sky state with the grace of a turkey vulture. I look down at my sweaty hands, which have left permanent indentations in the armrest. I am praying out loud, but my vows cannot be heard above the roar of the engine. All the passengers are in the same posture of fright, except for the woman directly in front of me, who is asleep, or dead. Either way she is lucky.

I have always been a cautious man. I avoid all activities that require a helmet. You won't catch me on a roller coaster, Ferris wheel, skateboard, horse, or ice skates. Crampons are not in my closet. Nor will you find me hugging a raft while negotiating white-water rapids. But now I am hurtling through space in a culvert with wings in the heart of high, buffeting winds.

We barely make it over the Mission Range peaks and then begin our descent into the windblown city of Great Falls. The plane somehow lands, and Rusty grants me permission to dash to the terminal restroom. Rusty himself does not look well.

Several passengers also rush down the slick portable stairs in an attempt to inhale as many cigarettes as possible in twenty minutes. One visibly shaking man says to me, "I don't know if I can get back on, man. Where's the nearest Greyhound station?"

On my way back to the plane, I pause at a gorgeous oil painting of what I believe to be the Lewis and Clark expedition. Oh, to be a pioneer on terra firma!

We reboard with all the enthusiasm of attending a wake. My white fingers find their familiar armrest indentations. The two props creak to life, and the plane taxis down the runway. Time to finger our rosaries and reflect on those big questions: Which wife is listed as the beneficiary on my life insurance policy? Did I unplug the coffeepot? Why didn't I drive?

I look down the aisle toward Rusty in search of reassurance. After all, he is our captain. He could perform last rites if necessary. I want to know if everything is going to be fine. As I start to speak, he reaches behind him and closes the curtain.

LUNCHTIME
IN IDAHO

A T THE MOSCOW, IDAHO, COMMUNITY CENTER, the Old Time Fiddlers play "You Picked a Fine Time to Leave Me, Lucille." Earl Lyon has the lead vocal and guitar, Clarence the melody line on the fiddle, and a recent widow, Ruth, is hammering out piano chords. Nobody in the band is under seventy years of age. They are having a blast.

The tables are set for fish sticks, green beans, fried potatoes, and fat, homemade peanut butter cookies, several of which I will take home with me. I spot Kay Simmons sitting at her usual spot. I lean down and give her a big hug. "How's my grandson?" she asks, burying her white hair in my chest.

"I'm great, Kay. How are you? Have you been golfing?" Kay, who holds the record in Moscow for longest fairway drive by a senior, adopted me last year. This hug is part of our weekly ritual. Hugs are the order of the day. In just an hour I will give and receive more than a dozen. No matter what my mood is, at the end of the lunch hour I am grinning like a jack-o'-lantern.

Friendly Neighbors Senior Citizens Program, a local volunteer group dedicated to helping seniors, puts the lunch on twice a week. The more fortunate people come to the community center. Many arrive in vans from area nursing homes. Some, like Kay, walk over from nearby apartments if the weather is good. I deliver lunches to people who cannot make the trip.

Diana, the cook, brings out the plastic cooler with cartons of 2 percent milk and a well-insulated box filled with hot meals and a pot holder. "Any changes?" I ask, looking over the address cards.

"Bonnie's in the hospital. She fell yesterday, so you can skip her. And Lafe's sister is visiting from Walla Walla, so there's two lunches for him. Oh, and could you pick up some fishing flies from him? Here's the money. And Mary wants you to give Irene this bundle of *National Enquirer*s."

When I drive up, I can see the outline of Lafe's wheelchair through the curtains in his door. Behind him I can see his sister cleaning the tiny house top to bottom as she does every three months. "Come on in, Dave," he calls, as I walk up. I've given up trying to correct him on my name. He hands me a plastic pill bottle filled with flies he has tied. I give him Diana's five dollars.

"What are you working on, Lafe?" Two large western saddles surround him.

"I'm putting new leather on these saddle horns." Lafe, a hemophiliac, always has a project that involves sharp instruments and leather. In addition to tying flies, he makes rifle scabbards, wallets, checkbooks, western belts, and key chains. When he nicks himself, it's off to the hospital. He never stops smiling. I'm relieved his sister is visiting.

The next stop is a little wood-frame house near the park. "Thelma?" I call, as I enter through the front door. (No one on my rounds locks their doors.) I walk through Thelma's house past the clutter—mostly paperwork from physicians, pharmacists, insurance companies, and others associated with the business of aging—calling her name from room to room and out the back door, where I find her in the garden among the waving hollyhocks and bright purple and lipstick-red bachelor buttons. She wears a wide-rimmed straw hat and below the brim a bigger smile than I thought possible given her 5-foot frame. She has on a plaid skirt above the knee, white socks, and a mustard-colored sweater despite the 80-degree temperature.

I hold her hand as I always do and I feel her ninety-six-year-old skin, wrinkly like an elephant's but buttery like a puppy's first coat. "Do I have to pay for these lunches?" she asks.

"No, Thelma. Mrs. Thompson paid for the whole month." We go through this routine every week. "Don't worry, Thelma. As long as I'm delivering, you will never have to pay for these lunches." She smiles, reassured, squeezes my hand, then goes back to her flowers.

A block away is Clara's house and immaculately kept lawn and rose garden. Clara is even smaller than Thelma, and her white hair is trimmed short with curls. When she goes downtown to the bank, she puts on high heels, lipstick and makeup, and a blouse and skirt.

Clara is ninety-two and has a thing for me. She flirts, puts her arm around my waist, and we shuffle along through the house to the kitchen, where I set down the lunch tray and put the pint of milk in the refrigerator next to some bottles of beer. "My mother would be mad at me for such a messy house!" she says. "But I hate to clean house. I'd much rather be outside. Wouldn't you?"

No one asks me why I volunteer. Maybe because the answer is too obvious: Clara's arm around my waist. Kay's hugs. Lafe's projects. Thelma's hand in mine. The big cookies, of course.

But there's one more reason.

When I return to the community center, a man is singing "Danny Boy" a cappella. Everyone has put their forks and knives down. I stand with my empty boxes at the entrance, not wanting to interrupt. Someone whispers to me: "This is the first time he has sung this song alone since his wife died last week. They used to sing together." The singer's voice is strong and steady. We hang on each note. His eyes are closed. For the moment he is not alone.

RELOCATION
REVISITED

E IGHTY-ONE-YEAR-OLD REI OSAKI is the last passenger off the 1:50 afternoon flight from Seattle. She descends a steep, portable staircase in the Palouse drizzle at the Moscow–Pullman Airport and pauses for a moment at the bottom of the wet stairs, looking for anything familiar.

We have never met face to face. All I have to go on is an old black-and-white photograph, a decade of letters and phones calls, and a story. The photograph was taken fifty-six years ago, the last time Rei Osaki (Kihara then) lived here as a University of Idaho law student during World War II. In 1943, the airport wasn't here. Neither were her brother or father. They were prisoners at Heart Mountain Relocation Camp in Wyoming. Rei's mother was in a mental institution, having suffered a nervous breakdown upon seeing her family "relocated" and their Yakima County farm in Washington State taken away forever.

The Kiharas were American citizens.

Despite such pressures, Rei, who now lives in Pasadena,

California, went on to graduate from the UI College of Law in 1943. She was the first Japanese American to graduate from the law school and the sixteenth woman in Idaho to become a lawyer. Now she is back for an alumni reunion.

I greet her with a hug and take her bags. "A half a century, Stephen. I never thought this day would come. When did you get this airport?"

My initial meeting with Rei was by phone in 1991, when I wrote an article about her experience. At the time she said, "I lost my home in Washington. I knew it was wrong, but I felt powerless to do anything about it. We wondered if the government would round up all the Japanese and kill us. I felt hope, though, because of the Constitution." Rei's father gave her the family cash and told her to put it in a bank, which she did upon arriving in Moscow for school. "I was the only one free," she says.

Even in Moscow, Idaho, where Rei was a student, racism was at a fevered pitch. An editorial in the local *Daily Idahonian* titled "Japanese into Idaho?" highlighted the cockeyed thinking of the times: "Idaho Gov. Chase A. Clark is quite perturbed at the thought that thousands of Japanese might be sent into Idaho and thus probably be competing with white Idahoans. For once here . . . they would multiply at a far greater rate . . . than the native white population."

For 110,000 Japanese Americans incarcerated during the war because of Executive Order 9066, the story was similar to Rei's. Homes, families, and livelihoods were ruined, and guaranteed constitutional rights were thrown out the window in the face of hysteria and the name of national security. Idaho had its own camp at Minidoka, where, at its peak, 9,861 Americans were held. Ten camps were built, nine in the West.

Set far away from population centers, these were dusty, makeshift places of plywood and tar paper. Yoshiko Uchida, a child of the camps and the author of *Desert Exile*, described her home in Topaz, Utah, as a "city of dust." Rei, who escaped the camps because she was a student, visited her family in Wyoming and described conditions as "stark, high altitude, thin air, very hot in the summer, very cold in the winter." To this day she refers to the relocation centers as "concentration camps."

When her father was released from Heart Mountain, he returned to Yakima County and started from scratch. In an odd turn of events, Rei's brother was inducted into the military and went overseas to defend the very country that had denied him his rights.

We spend the next two days trying to locate buildings that Rei might remember, but after fifty years only a couple remain. Our talk is mainly about families and current events, but the memory of those war years is still fresh. She remembers how her family burned a Japanese-American version of Shakespeare's writing for fear it would be seen as subversive. But she especially remembers her father's pain. To the day he died, she says, "He could never talk about it."

Rei has a fierce determination to make sure that relocation orders never occur again, working with the Japanese-American Citizens League to keep watch against hate crimes against Japanese Americans. During the first Gulf War, she was part of a group that monitored human rights abuses against Iraqis or anyone from the Middle East. She jokes that she is too liberal for her friends.

At the end of her stay I ask Rei how she managed to concentrate on her studies in the face of so many obstacles. She writes down this poem: "Do not forget / Inside the thicket there is / Blooming plum blossom."

A Vernacular of
Faith and Loss

*Faith is walking as far as the light
and taking one more step.*
—Sören Kierkegaard

WHITMAN COUNTY CHAPLAIN Ben Benthien pulls his Chevrolet Caprice sheriff's car over to the gravelly roadside shoulder and begins to weep. I squirm in my seat and look out the passenger window. Half-foot-high winter wheat and tender stalks of peas surround us on all sides. Meadowlarks and red-winged blackbirds settle and sing on some lone cattails between the vast rolling fields. Other drivers brake suddenly when they see the white police car, not because of the crying, but because they expect us to pull them over for speeding. We are not far from one of Ben's "memory spots," places that remind him where people have lost control, for one reason or another, of cars, trucks, and lives, and in an instant forever changed the order of some small western community.

Ben has many memory spots, mostly curves, bridges, and drop-offs on and around Highway 195 to Spokane, where there are clusters of fatalities every month, the type of gut-wrenching accidents driver education films feature in mostly failed attempts to keep teenagers from drinking and driving. No matter how many years pass, Ben still remembers each and every tragedy of alcohol, ice, and the inexplicable to last several lifetimes.

Around the eastern Washington wheat community of Colfax, the chaplain is called "Big Ben," or simply "Benthien." Most people in this county seat of 2,700 know Ben personally but would prefer to meet him in a neutral setting, like the Wheat 'n' Barley restaurant, over a bowl of lentil soup at lunch.

"I bring pain," Ben says.

For it's Chaplain Ben who appears like an apparition at horrific highway accidents carrying a Bible, looking rumpled in his customary black cowboy boots, shiny suit, and wide tie. And it's left to Ben to knock on the doors of the unsuspecting in the dreamy darkness of early morning, those unconscious hours when only bad news arrives. He's known for his bluntness, even criticized for it, but he wants the grieving process to begin immediately. "Your daughter has been in an accident. She is dead." Often he is asked to repeat every minute detail of the crash over and over again until the information sinks down to the place in the heart reserved for permanent hurt.

If it's a death notification of a suicide, Ben waits until the survivor is no longer alone, because the event can set off an "echo suicide." Sometimes the echo takes a while to resonate, as in the case of the eighty-seven-year-old woman who put the barrel of a handgun in her mouth and pulled the trigger—decades after her son had done the same thing with a shotgun. "That was strange. Older women never use guns," Ben says. "She was going to have to go to a nursing home, and I guess she didn't want to."

On the subject of suicide, Ben says, "Most people kill themselves because they have no blue skies. They only see black. Do you know what I mean?"

ALL MORNING WE'VE BEEN STOPPING at these memory spots, like the small concrete bridge built in 1931 off the exit into Thorton. "It was several years ago," Ben begins. "The weekend of the Apple Cup football game. I was called to a fatal accident here, where this guy had run into the side of the bridge. I walked up, and right away I knew him. He didn't like me, never did, or ministers in general. But I was always friendly to him.

"This was the first accident where I knew the victim real well. I was new on the job, but since then I've known a lot of people who have died."

CARNAGE IS A GOOD STARTING WORD in the vocabulary of what Ben witnesses. Loss is another. Also disbelief. Then again, perhaps there's no adequate vocabulary for what chaplains experience. That's why chaplains, along with police, soldiers, and physicians, have devised an entire vernacular to erect walls between what the mind knows and the heart feels. It's one more way to survive. A "possible" means a dead person. A "domestic" is a spousal beating that could result in a "possible." To describe the injuries of a crop duster who crashed last July in the tricky wind tunnels of the Snake River, Ben and Sheriff Steve Tomson switch to medical lingo. "He's got a broken C-1 and an L-3," meaning the pilot severed various parts of his neck and back.

A twisting Palouse hill just north of Steptoe. Another memory spot. "It was a single mom, her mother, and two twin five-year-old girls." I inhale, hold my breath, and cringe.

Ben continues but thankfully leaves out a few critical details. "They hit that guardrail over there. The helicopters took the adults away. The twins were strapped in the back seat and were OK." I exhale.

"I took the two girls to the hospital in Spokane; they were traumatized, so I gave 'em two red bears, and they held on to those bears the entire way; wouldn't even let go of them at the hospital."

None of this makes Chaplain Benthien cry this morning. Nor will he cry on the second to the last day of this same year, even though everyone else does—the EMTs, the nurses, the physicians, the parents—when six-year-old Amanda Pearson, named most inspirational player by Jennings Elementary School's first grade soccer team, falls out of her daddy's tractor near Chicken Flat Road and is killed instantly beneath the large back wheel.

No, the reason Ben is crying on this spring morning along this Palouse highway dotted with new crops and memory spots has to do with the reason he became an official Good Samaritan—specifically the ghost of Stephen Wade Benthien.

In 1968 Ben had finally taken the advice of a doctor and quit all that drinking from his Navy days. He was three years into a marriage with Linnea and worked in Portland as an insurance investigator. They weren't particularly religious then, but attending Baptist church services on Sundays was part of the social architecture they were building around their lives, and a growing influence on how they navigated their way through the world. Linnea was one month over-due with their second child when she went into labor. Ben remembers that day twenty-eight years ago like it happened this morning, remembers it in perfect slow-motion detail right down to the color and texture of the three yellow plas-tic chairs in the room where he waited for the news of his first son.

"The doctor comes in, sits down, and tells me the baby has died. He was born without a brain. Probably today doc-tors would have detected a problem beforehand. Up to that point in my life I had never had anyone close to me die, and I remember there was this guy sitting across from me in the room who comforted me and helped me through that moment.

"At 2:00 A.M. I was finally allowed to see Linnea. I remember walking down the hallway to her room, and there in the corridor I could hear Linnea and another woman—a black nurse—singing 'Amazing Grace.' I'll never forget that. I realized then and there we would be OK." They named their dead son Stephen Wade Benthien.

When Ben returned to the hospital the next day, the same man who had consoled Ben the previous night was still in the waiting room. "The guy says to me, 'I got hit harder than you did last night.'"

"How's that?" Ben asked.

"My baby lived, but my wife died."

They held on to each other and cried and cried and cried.

"Here I lost a baby that I had never held or seen. But he lost his wife. Through that experience God taught us how to deal with death." Ben would never see the man again or ever learn his name.

That moment, in the arms of a stranger, Ben realized how he wanted to spend the rest of his life. After four years of training at the New Tribes Mission in Rochester, Pennsylvania, he went to work in the Philippines as a missionary, spreading religion to what he called "unreached tribes in Satan's territory." After that, he served stints as pastor in Cascade, Idaho, and eastern Washington, and one in Darby, Montana, that went sour.

After telling me the story, Ben wipes his eyes with his bare fingers, clears the fog from his glasses with a handkerchief, shifts the sheriff's car into drive, and we coast into Rosalia, past a windowless cinder block Baptist church where he was once pastor. Whatever awkwardness there was between us was left behind on the highway shoulder. He looks over at me with a smile and asks, "Do you have any children?"

⁂

DRIVING INTO COLFAX TO MEET BEN that day, I read the daily message posted on the signboard at Huber Action Freight: "Faith is not a leap in the dark." But faith, the kind chaplains rely on, the kind Amanda's parents had in the waiting room at Colfax Hospital when, after the doctor told them the news, and Ben held their hands to say a word of prayer, the father, his shirt covered with his daughter's blood, said, "We believe she's with God. She's an angel now," this kind of unrelenting faith has always been a mystery to me.

I was brought up without religion, without a set of age-old truths to live by and fall back on in difficult times. I've dabbled in trendy Native American readings, in Zen and the art of everything, including ten Anthony Robbins tapes on how to put more power in my life for $150 plus postage. I've tried guided meditation and received a headache. A counselor of questionable credentials tried to get me to shout, but I couldn't. Jogging works sometimes. Espresso used to. And I've made a few failed attempts at organized religion, including one in Chicago, when I was sixteen, that worshiped Satan.

But for all my misgivings, I realize that I am missing

something. I see what faith communities do and the role they play in this country. A church can represent fellowship and social action within a broader circle of community. Prayers do seem to get answered. I have seen this firsthand in the waiting room of Sacred Heart Hospital when a friend made a miraculous—and that's the only word for it—recovery from a brain aneurysm. And there is no more joyful moment than singing hymns together in a church with good acoustics (although the hymns are often in unattainable keys). At the middle age of forty-something, surrounded on all sides by my own generation's cynicism and hyperindividualism, within the surreal marinade of a media-induced noise factory, I could use a little more fellowship and community. So maybe I should not have been surprised to find myself sitting in a sheriff's car with more than a little fear watching a fifty-four-year-old devout Baptist weep, while on the radio the dispatcher called, "Steptoe to Chaplain One. Steptoe to *Chaplain One*. Do you copy? Over."

During one of my faith-seeking periods last year I attended the Albion, Washington, Community Church's annual Thanksgiving Potluck, but as a musician, not a member, invited by Pastor Bill Lyons (no relation) to accompany his banjo with my guitar. After pie and coffee, we set up folding chairs in the dining hall and led a spirited sing-a-long to "Skip to My Lou," "Shortnin' Bread," and

"You Are My Sunshine." I saw people I usually don't rub up against in my small circle: an oil truck driver, retirees, farmers, three generations of a family eating together. Afterwards, I met Ben, who introduced himself as I was in the sanctuary packing up to leave.

It was a late Thanksgiving afternoon, soft autumn slant light fading all too quickly, and Ben's belly was full of turkey and fixings and two different kinds of pie. Despite a warm, open smile, right away when you look into Ben's blue eyes you can sense that he's seen more than the rest of us. Hidden behind the steel-rimmed glasses that Ben pushes constantly back up his nose with his index finger, his eyes have a tendency to absorb sadness and store it below in large bags. Extra-large, he fills any room no matter what the size—church or jail cell. His hands and ears are enormous, and he can't seem to get comfortable in a chair. He's like the kid in grade school you saw out of the corner of your eye jiggling his legs to some hidden rhythm. He's more at ease moving, especially in a car. An office boxes him in, keeps him off the streets where the action is, where people might need him.

AFTER TWO DECADES IN THE PASTORATE, Ben started the Whitman County chaplaincy program in the fall of 1989, leaving his post as minister in Rosalia for a full-time job without dependable pay. A move like that could only be labeled "a calling." Ben would be on permanent call twenty-four hours a day, seven days a week, in the service of those whose problems eclipsed his own: in hospital waiting rooms and jail cells, living rooms and kitchens and doorways, coffee shops and churches and street corners, and in the backs of ambulances. He would be at the vortex of every small-town catastrophe, of which there are many. His specialty as chaplain, with assistance from Linnea, would be comforting families who lose children.

His experience was limited to an intervention skills seminar the year before and a two-day training in Yakima. Sheriff Steve Tomson asked him to become chaplain to help his own officers who increasingly suffered burnout from performing dual duties of accident cleanup and death notification. Officers needed someone to counsel the victims and survivors so they could attend to the accident itself. Ben contends, however, that "the most important part of my job is comforting officers and firefighters and their families. Unfortunately, most of my time is spent keeping couples from killing each other."

Officers' vulnerabilities surface all the time, but the public rarely sees them. Ben recalls one officer who refused to leave a fatal traffic accident victim on a two-lane highway because the dead woman wore the same perfume as his wife, who was at that moment studying in England. After lengthy and delicate negotiations, the officer was finally coaxed into letting the coroner remove the woman's body.

Chaplains, many of them volunteers, exist in most communities in America. One hundred and fifty of them gathered in Oklahoma City in the aftermath of the Alfred P. Murrah Federal Building bombing to help counsel cleanup crews. Washington State does not pay chaplains out of its coffers because of laws defining separation of church and state, specifically, the First Amendment, and Article 1, Section 11 of the state constitution, which prohibits the use of public money for religious activities. Although no public funds officially support the Whitman County chaplaincy program, the sheriff's department does provide Ben with a car and gas, a phone, and a cramped 8-foot-by-4-foot office that he shares with the DARE enforcement officer. Health insurance is Ben's responsibility. Ben raises his own salary—around $25,000 in a good year—through contributions at churches and civic organizations. He supplements his income by occasionally preaching at the Country Bible Church, which in return lets Ben, Linnea, and their three dogs live rent free in the parsonage, a mile or so south of Dusty.

"We have a little savings, not a lot," he tells me. "I'm concerned about it, but every time we put a little away, something comes up. I'm not so naive to think God will provide, as God also wants us to do our part." When I tell him I think they have done their part, he blushes and says, "I don't know about that."

A case heard in the Washington State Supreme Court challenged the chaplaincy programs statewide. An ACLU–Washington lawsuit contended that the use of public funds in Pierce County ($30,000 in twelve years) to support religious counseling of persons not in a corrections facility or in institutional care violated the separation of church and state. Doug Honig from the ACLU said a significant portion of the Tacoma–Pierce County chaplains' job was proselytizing. The chaplain who directs the program refers to it as a "Christian ministry," and no non-Christian denominations are represented by the chaplains.

When I ask Ben about the lawsuit, he contradicts the ACLU's findings. "Pierce County has a rabbi and a Catholic priest available for counseling," he says. I ask him if they also have a Buddhist monk, just in case. I can tell by his body language that he doesn't consider my question funny. If the court rules in favor of the ACLU, Ben would likely lose his car, gas money, phone, office, and, no doubt, the chaplaincy program. But that didn't happen. In the summer of 1997 the Washington Supreme Court ruled in favor of chaplains.

Ben's side of the office is more clutter than usable floor

space. The office is just a rest stop where Ben drinks black coffee, checks his voice mail, and listens to the dispatcher's reports broadcast over a loudspeaker throughout the sheriff's office. The walls surrounding his desk are covered with pencil sketches of a bull elk, a doe and fawn, and a coyote; a calendar, courtesy of Farm Credit Services in Colfax; and a bulletin board with dozens of colorful shoulder patches from law enforcement departments in the United States and Canada. Among the departments are Texarkana, Texas, and Texarkana, Arkansas; Thunder Bay; Kitsap County, Washington; Court Officer, State of New York; State of Hawaii; the Border Patrol; and Ville de Québec.

A statement from Romans 13:4 hangs above his phone: "The policeman is sent by God to help you. But if you are doing something wrong, of course you should be afraid, for He will have you punished. He is sent by God for that very purpose." Above his green metal desk is this notice: "Due to budget constraints, the light at the end of the tunnel will be off until further notice." On the office door is the acronym GREAT, which stands for Gang Resistance Education and Training.

The desk has six drawers and a typewriter ledge, but no typewriter or computer. On top of the desk are pictures of Linnea, two boxes of Kleenex, a stapler, Rolodex, tape, books, and one of the stuffed red bears. Books include *When Self-Help Fails*, by Paul Quinnett, *The NIV* (New International Version) *Study Bible, A Guide to Crime Victim Services in the State of Washington*, and a couple of copies of a paperback titled *More Than a Carpenter*, by Josh McDowell. The back cover blurb reads, "In *More Than a Carpenter* Josh focuses upon the person who changed his life—Jesus Christ. It is a hardheaded book for people who are skeptical about Jesus' deity, his resurrection, his claims on their lives." After my second visit to Ben's office, a visit that included confessing my ambivalence about faith during lunch at Arby's, he gave me this book as a gift.

Besides the desk, there is a large, brown Naugahyde chair, a filing cabinet, and a typewriter stand where the phone sits. When Ben and I visit in the office between rides, our knees almost touch.

Down a short corridor and to the right is the break room where Ben refills his coffee cup. On the bulletin board hangs twenty-one Polaroid snapshots of the area's worst teenagers. Most are males. Beneath each face in handwriting lists a name, date of arrest, city of residency, and the crime. Burglary. Child rape. Assault 4. MIP (minor in possession). Residential burglary. Some of the teenagers have more than one crime beneath their name. Ben tells me the photos were taken at the time of arrest. Most of the teenagers try to look tough, but one kid is grinning. Underneath his name is written "child molester," and he lives in the town where I live. He looks familiar.

On the job Ben carries a can of pepper spray, and he is trained to secure an officer's firearm if the officer is injured. He recently purchased, because of threats from angry wife beaters, a .38 police special handgun, which he leaves at home. And because he is often away at night and his nearest neighbor is 2 miles away, he has taught Linnea how to use the gun. "I've been cussed out in courtrooms, the hallways of the sheriff's office, and in the street. I never had a hand-gun until I became a chaplain. I do trust God, but, at the same time, I keep a gun at the house."

Within minutes of our introduction in Albion, Ben told me stories of his job—mostly about abused women in rural areas, anchored by fear and isolation from leaving their hus-bands and boyfriends: "I can walk into a church to talk about the chaplaincy program and look out among the faces and instantly tell who's been abused. Usually when I men-tion abuse all the women's heads drop, and the men look up and glare at me."

He once approached such a woman and asked, "How often do you get beat up?"

"I'm dealing with it," the woman replied, beginning to cry.

"How well are you dealing with it?" She rushed away to join her husband outside the church. Ben never saw her again.

On and off during the next year I rode with Ben on his rounds. He introduced me to prison trustees, nurses aides, highway workers, detectives, waitresses, and janitors as a writer interested in chaplains. When we weren't waiting for tragedies, we rode around the 2,159-square-mile county, prayed together with hospital patients, drank iced tea in country cafes, and dropped in on elderly shut-ins. (A sheriff's car, by the way, is the safest place on earth to be. You are invincible, and you can drive as fast as you want.) During our conversations, I learned the subject of spousal abuse is Ben's greatest passion. He has served on the Alternatives to Violence board and led women to the local safe house on numerous occasions. I also realized that Ben would only talk about his faith if I asked him directly. My favorite saying of his is "I'm not so heavenly minded that I can't be of earthly good."

In one of his monthly columns in the *Colfax Gazette,* Ben writes, "Love is to cross all barriers: economical, political, racial, religious, gender, and any other barrier that man is capable of building. To love someone doesn't mean we have to like a person's actions. It simply means that we are to accept them as a fellow human being and be willing to come alongside whenever they need us."

One day, between rides, I ask him if religion ever contributes to abuse, or at least prevents women from seeking help. "Ministers will often tell women not to leave," he says. "They quote 1 Peter 13:1." Ben turns around and plucks a Bible off the stack of books behind him. He quickly finds the passage and begins to read, "The wife should submit to the husband, who is not saved, may be saved by her actions."

He shuts the book and says, "As you read the Scriptures, women were not beat up. The Scriptures do not teach that a man has to have a woman under his thumb. Ministers who teach that are wrong. The church is finally starting to look at domestic violence more and more. For years they had blinders on. I've had women ask me, 'Is it a sin to leave a husband who beats me?' I tell them, 'It's a sin not to.' They say, 'If he kills me, it must be God's way.' Now, I'm as religious as anyone, and I'm sure God wouldn't want that."

ANOTHER MORNING VISIT TO BEN, another message at Huber's Freight: "Faith is believing I am useful to God." Linnea joins us for lunch at the Wheat 'n' Barley from her job as secretary at the Colfax Baptist Church. We sit near the back, where fifteen women recite the Pledge of Allegiance to open a meeting. Linnea is a big-boned woman with a smile that won't quit. They have been married for thirty-one years and have two grown children, Michael and Katherine. Unlike Ben, who tries unsuccessfully to avoid listening to hard-luck stories when he eats lunch, Linnea seeks them out. Within minutes the busboy is at our table bringing Linnea up to date on the status of his wife's health and other intimate details of his life. I can tell by Ben's sudden interest in his iceberg lettuce salad that he would rather be somewhere else—like back in the car.

One of the biggest concerns for chaplains is burnout from being on permanent call. During Easter dinner a few years ago, Ben was called to a suicide. Christmas Eve is routinely a time of increased highway fatalities and spousal abuse. Three years ago, as the entire family celebrated his daughter's birthday at the Olive Garden restaurant in Spokane, his beeper went off, and within an hour and a half he was notifying forty-five sorority members at Washington State University that one of their sisters was dead. When Ben vacations he doesn't like to mingle or talk to anyone. And it's not unusual when he returns for a call to be waiting for him as he steps off the plane. "I need to get away sometimes or I will burn out very quickly," he says apologetically.

He's also decided to limit the number of times he will counsel couples. "I try to avoid a long-term commitment. Five or six times is all. If they still need help, I send them elsewhere. I don't have the time. Sometimes couples are required by law to seek counseling, but they have no money. I'm the only freebie on the block."

The busboy picks up his plastic tray and moves on. Linnea returns to us and without missing a beat picks up on the subject of burnout and stress. She begins to discuss last year's hunting season, and Ben says, "Please, let's not talk about it. I still haven't worked it out with myself." Then, after a meaningful look from Linnea that says where they have drawn the line in the sand after three decades of marriage, he relents: "OK, you can tell him."

Linnea recalls that, just before the start of deer season, Ben decided he wasn't going hunting. "I looked at him to see if he was sick," she tells me. "He's been a hunter for twenty-five years. He's always loved to go out in the woods with his buddies."

Ben couldn't figure out why either until he bumped into the county coroner, Pete Martin, who had also given up the sport. "He said that he just couldn't deal with any more blood and guts," Ben said. That made sense to Ben. He'd finally seen too much: "Maybe I might go pheasant hunting, but I don't know."

✒ ✒

TODAY AT HUBER'S, "FAITH IS DRAWING on God's grace."

When I arrive at the jail on a Monday, I'm ushered into the under-sheriff's office that Ben has taken over for a tense counseling session. The first words I hear from Ben as I walk in are "I'm trying to prevent you guys from hurting each other."

This time the "guys" are a small woman, who sits with every appendage crossed, and a slight-looking man swiveling around and around in the deputy sheriff's chair with an unmistakable smirk on his face and playing with a pen. The woman, let's call her Maria, has been living with the man, Marty, for nine months. They have one child together. They are not married, although Maria would like to be. Marty says he has no intention of ever marrying. Her accent surprises me, and I later learn she is from Armenia. On Sunday she pushed Marty into a wall. Pushed him hard, Marty says, still smirking. She was arrested on a domestic abuse charge. In the last six months the police have gone out to their place in the country three times, once on a suicide attempt by Maria, an attempt Ben says was "a cry for help." She took a handful of Tylenol and Tums and got a bad stomachache.

Among their many problems are two kids who have arrived for the summer from Marty's two failed marriages.

They have been rude to Maria and disruptive in general. One of the kids, thirteen-year-old Robert, waits on the long oak bench in the lobby, absorbed in a comic book. Ben suggests that Maria leave for a week of "cooling off," but she refuses after Marty says the baby must stay with him. Marty also mentions how he'd like to take a strap to Robert's thighs like he used to, but "you guys would have me arrested." He also prefers the way his neighbor dealt with his son: "He threw him up against the wall and told him he'd kick his ass if he ever misbehaved like that again.

"He hasn't had any trouble since," Marty finishes, looking over at me for approval. I look down at my notebook.

Maria, for her part, sighs and says, "I just don't know what to do." After an hour the couple leaves with nothing resolved except another appointment with Ben later in the week.

Ben and I discuss the situation on our way to the Dusty Cafe for iced teas. He is exasperated and realistic. "There's nothing short of a miracle from God to change their situation. What you just saw is typical of 70 percent of what I deal with: when children are not really the top priority." He noticed Marty's smirk, too, and the references to violence. A few weeks later he will tell me the counseling accomplished nothing.

When we return to the office, I ask him about his survival mechanisms.

He can't let the misery stick, he says. To show me how he copes, he picks up a Bible and places it on his shoulder. He points to the book. "Let's say this is Stephen Lyons. When I am finished dealing with you, I put this book back. Then I pick up Marty's problems. I try to forget everything previous. I tell my wife that if I tried to carry twenty Bibles on my shoulders I'd be burned out. There would be no way I could do the job."

To survive certain deaths, nothing seems to work. He carries a photo of Dana, a much beloved Colfax High School student who, on her way back from a music lesson in Pullman, didn't make the curve where Highway 195 intersects Prune Orchard Road. Her face was so badly disfigured that officers on the scene could not make a positive identification. Ben could. Minutes later he made the death notification to her parents, who had heard the sirens from their house in town.

"She is the only person that I carry a photo of. I don't know why I do it. Maybe to remind me that bad things happen to good people. And she was one of the good ones." He pulls his chaplain's baseball cap down low so I can't see his eyes. "I've only had three or four like that in eight years. Now that's not so bad, is it?"

ON THE NORTHEAST CORNERSTONE of the Country Bible Church in eastern Washington is the inscription "St. John's Congregational Church 1926." The church, which sits in a cradle of rolling wheat fields off Highway 127 to Walla Walla, must be older than 1926 because a plaque inside the sanctuary lists all the ministers in chronological order beginning in 1908. Most of the names are German. After 1988 the list is blank. The church used to be strict. Women who wore above-the-knee dresses were asked to leave. Until the 1960s, Country Bible was German-speaking. This last bit of history came from Bernice, the pianist for Country Bible and a lifetime member of the congregation, who is writing a history of the town of Dusty, 5 miles to the north. Next year Bernice will move to a nursing home in Colfax, where she plans to finish the history. Her musical interpretation of "Sweet Hour of Prayer" is exceptional.

The exterior of the church is simple, white-framed, with maybe ten windows. The upper fifth of the windows are stained glass in a swirly, multicolored pattern. The lower four-fifths are stained in a style used on frosted bathroom windows. Ancient hardwood trees—rare in this part of the Palouse—ring one side of a gravel parking lot that had five cars on the day I attended services.

My wife, Jan, and I were invited as special guests to the church by Ben. Country Bible has no official minister, and Ben fills in about twice a month. It was a cold, blustery day toward the end of the summer, one of those days when you realize another season is starting. I had been riding with Ben in his sheriff's cruiser off and on for about four months, and we had become good friends. When I said I wanted to see him in action at the church, he made a day of it, extending an invitation for dinner following the service. We accepted. He insisted that we bring nothing to the dinner, but Jan brought zucchini bread.

A short staircase leads to the small sanctuary. Pews divide into three sections on a slight slope. The largest number of pews is in the middle section. Hymnals and Bibles nest in front of the pews. Furnishings are scarce. There are no cross, statues, or oil paintings of Jesus, nothing, in fact, to indicate a church. An appendage to the sanctuary is a crying room with a large window looking out over the rows of pews. Inside the room is a crib, some toys, a bookshelf crammed with books, and a large rocking chair. A speaker sits inside, just above the window, so mothers with crying children won't miss the sermon. A huge floral arrangement filled the space in front of the lectern from which Ben spoke. A ceiling fan whirred above Ben, and an amber lamp lit the reading surface of the lectern.

On the Sunday we attended the Country Bible Church, there were eleven people in the center section of pews and eight in the left section. The right section was empty. In the center section sat the crop duster pilot who had crashed his plane earlier in the summer near Wawawai, Washington, after experiencing tricky wind sheers off the Snake River canyon. He broke several vertebrae in his back and possibly in his neck, and was wearing a medical device called a halo, prompting Ben, who never passes up an opportunity to make a joke, to comment, "I see someone's already got his halo." The halo is stainless steel and holds his head in place in such a way that his eyes permanently look skyward as if watching for another plane to drop. The metal points of the halo appear driven directly into his skull, pushing up his eyelids and giving him a frightened look. Brownish goo oozes out from the two points. The pilot could have easily died from the crash, but instead he crawled for a mile across a pea field to a county road, where a woman on her way to work at Washington State University found him. Country Bible held a prayer chain for a week while he was in intensive care in Spokane.

On the day he crashed, I was drinking iced tea with Ben at the Dusty Cafe. A Washington Department of Transportation worker who knew the pilot and said he wasn't surprised by the accident joined us. "I would never fly with him," he said, shaking his head and grinning. "I've seen some of his landings."

The transportation worker went on to tell us that a big road construction project over in Idaho would eventually create a five-lane road with a bike path. He also rattled off the number of vehicles per hour on the I–5 freeway in Tacoma versus the number of vehicles moving past the cafe on Highway 26. There is, of course, considerable difference. After we finished our iced teas we took our glasses and spoons into the kitchen and placed them in the sink. The transportation employee asked the waitress what the special would be that evening. She said pork chops with apple sauce. Five ninety-five.

In the left section of church pews were the wife, mother-in-law, and father-in-law of the western singer Wylie Gustafson of Wylie and the Wild West Show. (Bernice, the piano player and historian, is Wylie's grandmother.) Wylie had just signed a recording contract with Rounder Records and was not at church that day. Instead, he was relaxing in Alaska with his buddies. Wylie is known for his yodeling. His wife, Kim, told the congregation that he would be performing in October at the Coeur d'Alene Tribal Bingo/Casino just outside Worley, Idaho, and that even though she did not know the exact date, we were certainly welcome to attend. The bingo hall is a new destination for a wide variety of musical acts, including a stop on Ray Price's comeback tour. Later in the fall they'll sponsor "the return of women's boxing," which will feature Helga "Snowcat" Risoy, fighting for the Northwest Women's Welterweight Title. The matchmaker is Moe Smith. Fights are sanctioned under the supervision of the Idaho Boxing Commission, and in fine print the advertisements state, "Fighters may change without notice."

This is what Ben wore when he looked out at nineteen parishioners (twenty if you count Bernice) and began the service by declaring, "It's a good day to serve the Lord." A white, short-sleeved, snap-button shirt cut in a western style, and a gray-and-black sports jacket, also western cut. Matching gray pants covered his black cowboy boots, but more often than not one cuff snagged on the top of a boot. Around the wide collar of his shirt hung a bolo tie set off by a pewter-colored soaring eagle.

Linnea wore a black dress with gold-colored buttons down the front, dark hose, and flaming red high heels. She beamed at her husband during the service. She would later sing a religious ballad, "Majesty," accompanied by a 2-foot-tall karaoke machine that worked beautifully, accompanying Linnea with a string orchestra and full chorus. (During "Majesty," Bernice left the piano and sat in the front row of pews.) Because the congregation is too small to have a choir, Linnea led in the singing of the hymns. When it was time for announcements, Linnea asked us to pray for a missionary friend of theirs who had been stricken with cancer in New Guinea, as she put it, "in Satan's territory."

The only other announcement was Ben's, inviting everyone concerned about Country Bible to stay after service next Sunday to discuss the future of the church. Ben had told me privately that he wanted some clarification as to his role. He isn't looking to be the church's permanent minister, but if they decided they wanted him, he would take on the job even though he is on call seven days a week as county chaplain. He wears two beepers: one for the sheriff's office, the other to keep him in touch with the Colfax Volunteer Fire Department. Attendance at the church has been slipping of late, down to nine one Sunday. Older parishioners have died, and many of the young families that might replace them travel instead to Colfax or Pullman, bigger towns with larger congregations. Ben believes the church can win them back with a full-time minister. One of the activities Ben would like to bring back is a coffee hour following the service so people could mingle and visit. He would like a Sunday school, too, but there were no children at this service. Ben is paid $100 per service, twice the going rate, he says. For funerals, Ben doesn't charge for his services, but sometimes he'll receive a donation of around $15.

Linnea sat with a parishioner named Jim in the second

row of the left section. He is in his thirties and used to attend a fundamentalist church but got "stung real bad," Linnea says. *Stung* meant he had a terrible experience at the church and was only now "coming back to the Lord." I never found out what happened. Jim also had a "special lady" in his life, a mother of two who was dying from brain seizures. Jim had met her as part of his job in assisting hospice patients. During the service Jim and Linnea shared a hymnal, but each had their own Bibles.

Linnea expresses her faith differently than Ben, who tends to be low-key. Linnea refers to "the Lord" frequently in conversation: "The Lord is bringing Jim back to us." "The Lord is teaching us patience." "We're not doing anything. It's the Lord doing it!" In this part of the West, where New Age faiths can sometimes overshadow traditional religions, her public devotion seems straight out of a Bible Belt church in the South.

She also smiles nonstop. The only time I have seen Linnea not smile was at this year's Albion Community Church's Thanksgiving potluck. She had brought her karaoke machine and wanted to sing three songs, but the minister requested, "Could you just sing two? We have a lot going on today." During her first song she forgot the lyrics of the second verse and just stood there smiling at us and swaying until the machine's orchestra came around to the third verse.

Like Ben, Linnea worries about her weight. I have been with her at several meals, and she does not use salt or sugar, but she did eat at least two slices of Jan's zucchini bread. Ben has lost 30 pounds this summer by taking a pill that suppresses his appetite and walking his dogs 2 miles every morning. His golden retriever, a descendant of former president Gerald Ford's golden retriever, sleeps under the front porch. Before Ben and Linnea and the dogs moved in, coyotes regularly napped on the porch.

I followed the sequence of the service by glancing at the program, which had a sketch of Country Bible Church on the cover with the phrase "Holding Forth the Word of Life." Rising up above the church in the sketch were dramatic cumulus storm clouds, the kind we almost never experience in eastern Washington. The back of the program was blank except for the words "Sermon Notes." The inside front cover gave the name of the church, the date, and the following order of events: Prelude; Hymn No. 418, "All Your Anxiety"; Scripture Reading; Moment for Missions; Pre-Prayer Meditation; Morning Prayer; Announcements; Offertory; Hymn No. 419, "Abide with Me"; Message: Ben Benthien; Hymn No. 420, "Only Believe"; Benediction; and Postlude. The hymns, the pre-prayer meditation, the morning prayer, the benediction, and the postlude, all had asterisks next to them, indicating that the congregation should stand at those times. During the service, Hymn No. 418, "All Your Anxiety," was replaced by Hymn No. 419, "Abide with Me." No reason was given for the switch.

The Scripture reading was from James 4: "What causes wars, and what causes fightings among you? You desire and do not have; so you kill. And you covet and cannot obtain; so you fight and wage war. . . . Unfaithful creatures!" As Ben read from a Bible wrapped in a custom leather cover, his version was different from the verses I was reading in one of the church's Bibles. Mostly the differences were in the choice of adjectives and verbs. Desire became covet. Then covet became want. Unfaithful became adulterous.

On Ben's home computer is a Bible software package that can prepare sermons with the touch of a button. However, this sermon felt improvised and, as it unfolded over the next hour, customized to include all of us. Twice Ben referred to me directly—three times if you count his introduction. Once was in reference to the sentence "Therefore whoever wishes to be a friend of the world makes himself an enemy of God." "If I say that Stephen is my friend and then I stab him in the back, then I'm not a real Christian," Ben said. The second time Ben mentioned my name was in the recounting of a counseling session he mediated that didn't go well. "Stephen was there!" Ben shouted, pointing at me for confirmation. I looked around, smiled, and nodded at Wiley's family. Wiley's wife smiled back.

At the offering, which Wylie's father-in-law collected, two blue velvet bags held with wooden handles were passed around. They reminded me of Crown Royal whiskey bags. I dropped in a folded dollar bill. After the service, I saw the bags on a table next to a rubbery bank deposit purse with the zipper across the top. Ben, who never handles the collection money, said the Country Bible Church has a good-size nest egg, somewhere in the $20,000 range, left a few years ago by a local parishioner who willed the church some Washington farmland that was sold to create the nest egg.

After the service, the injured pilot buttonholed me in the church parking lot. Despite the halo and the obvious pain, the man was lively and chatty, telling me he hoped to soon fly a plane he owned from the airport in Pullman out to Colfax, "to see how it felt," and to be crop dusting by spring. All of this was said just out of earshot of his wife, who was trying with some difficulty to lock up the church. In a typically understated western drawl, the man summed up his experience by saying, "Yeah, that was some deal. Caught me by surprise."

No message today at Huber's as I coast into Colfax, but I notice the electronic signboard above the Farm Credit Services lists the current price of wheat at $5.04 a bushel. Wheat farmers are going to clean up this year. I am careful not to exceed the speed limit, although since riding with Ben, I have met enough policemen to feel somewhat protected. I've even developed a fantasy. If I am stopped, they will recognize me and say, "Oh, you're the writer—Ben's friend." Then they would let me go with a warning.

My other fantasy is that Ben will knock on *my* door in the middle of the night.

When I arrive at the jail, I can sense bad news.

"We've had a lot of tragedy this past week," Ben says. "Did you hear about Jesse?"

Jesse Persons is a senior at Colfax High School, a dream son with a 4.0 grade point average, student body president, a shoo-in for class valedictorian, wrestler and football player for the Colfax Bulldogs, and a devout Christian. On a sweltering August afternoon at 3:00 P.M., he was "driving truck" for a local farmer during wheat harvest. While waiting for his next load of grain, he walked down a hill to assist Ed, a middle-aged man who was fixing a broken axle on a combine. The clutch on Jesse's Dodge grain truck popped out.

104

"He put it in third instead of first," Ben said, and the grain truck just rolled down on the combine and the two men.

"Imagine," Ben says, "thousands of acres of land for that truck to roll through, and what does it do? It hits both of them." The truck hit the combine, which then rolled over Jesse and broke his back. Ed's leg was broken in five places, and he would undergo three operations. On the way to the hospital in Spokane the EMTs told Jesse he could cuss if he wanted to, but he refused.

Jesse is 5 feet 4, 150 pounds, and would spend the next six weeks in the hospital. Everyone in Colfax closely monitored his progress. A few weeks after the accident, two jail trustees helping Ben unload a van were even discussing Jesse.

"How's the kid the combine rolled on?"

"I heard on the news he's got some tingling in his arm."

Doctors are skeptical if he will ever walk again, but Jesse is determined. In an article by Dave Trimmer in the sports section of the *Spokesman Review* on October 31 of that year, Jesse summed up his experience in terms of faith:

> I was kind of high in my faith. Satan kind of does things to you when you get high enough. He kind of knocks you down to see if you're truly up there or if it is just a facade. I was on my way

up and he tried to knock me down, but it isn't going to work.

I was near death. There was probably a point where He could have taken me or kept me here, and He kept me here. It changed my outlook on people. I'm not too big now to do something, to tell somebody what I feel, or to show emotion. . . . It feels good. I think people should do it all the time. The world would be a better place.

On this day in August, however, Jesse's condition was unknown. Ben is restless and suggests we go pay Ed a visit at the small hospital in Colfax. He has a present for Ed's wife, Rosie. On the drive up to the hospital Ben tells me more about the past week: "We found a guy in the field who had been dead three days. From a heart attack. He lived alone, so no one reported him missing. Didn't even hire extra help during harvest. He cut the wheat, loaded it, and hauled it to town all by himself. Somebody finally saw his combine on a hill and noticed it hadn't moved for a few days. He hadn't been feeling well that week, according to people at the machine shop where he bought some parts." His mother, who lived nearby, might have noticed the absence of her son, but as Ben says, "She is senile, or at least that's how I would describe her."

Ben had driven out in a four-wheel-drive pickup with a deputy, and "as we came up, I could see him lying there in the field." The temperatures that week had been in the nineties. "You can imagine what that was like."

I ask Ben if dead bodies disturb him. "No, I've seen a lot of death. I'd rather go out and find a body than visit a nursing home any day. The body is only a dwelling place for the spirit. But we were lucky that the wind was blowing the other way."

Ben's week also included a death notification that went bad. "We had a woman die of natural causes, and we went in two police cars to notify her daughter, who lives in a trailer park in Pullman." The daughter met them outside the trailer, and when Ben asked if they could come inside to tell her something important, she turned belligerent and refused. "I like to give notifications in the homes so people can sit down," he said. When Ben finally told her about the death of her mother, she almost passed out. She called later and apologized and asked Ben to perform the funeral service.

When we park at the Whitman Hospital and Medical Center, I watch Ben pull out a crisp $100 bill from his wallet and slip it in into his pocket. A work release prisoner in coveralls with a rake spots Ben and walks over to the car. Ben asks him how many times he's been to alcohol treatment since his arrest. "Three times," the man says. "And I'm on my way to the VA hospital in Spokane for a three-week stay." I can tell he likes Ben, and Ben respects him enough to be honest: "You know, you're a nice guy when you're not drunk." After the prisoner leaves, Ben says, "He's been going to church but not using it. When he gets drunk, he gets mean. He beat up his girlfriend."

As with all our trips to the hospital, Ben begins his rounds by stopping at the nurses' station and glancing at the chart. The nurses and aides always tease him, but they also turn to Ben when the stress is unbearable. During one visit a nurse came up to Ben and announced, "I just crashed." Ben immediately took her arm, and they disappeared for a half hour into an empty room.

In one of those small-town coincidences, it turned out the nurse's mother was only two doors away, recovering from a nasty fall she suffered because of the flu. We visit her next. Ben asks if he could pray for her. She agrees. Ben bows his head. It feels awkward, but I do the same. "Lord, I pray that you would undertake for Pauline that she'd be able to recover from her flu and her fall," Ben says quietly. "Give wisdom to all the doctors and nurses as they administer to her physical needs. God, I also ask that you administer to her special needs. In Jesus' name, Amen."

Next we walk into an elderly patient's room just as she is

coughing violently and spitting up clear phlegm. Ben wipes her mouth and calls in a nurse. At another stop the conversation goes like this:

"How are you today?"

"Not very good."

"I'm Ben Benthien, the hospital chaplain. Anything we can do for you?"

"You can find me a rich man."

We locate Ed's room and meet his wife, Rosie, in the hallway. She works at Arby's in Pullman. From his room we can hear Ed moaning in pain. Ben introduces me as "a friend," and then, with his palm turned down discreetly, hands her the hundred-dollar bill. He won't tell her who it's from, and I get the feeling she thinks the money is from me. Rosie's eyes fill. She looks down at the floor, with the money rolled up in her hand. Ben tells her, "The Bible teaches us to receive as well as give." She looks up and tells us of all the cards and flowers Ed has received "from people we don't even know." I can see she has that present tense energy found in hospital corridors and waiting rooms. She lives from minute to minute, test result to test result. Ed will pull through, she says, but it will take months of painful healing. And a lot of faith.

For most of us, a day like this one would be an aberration. "A bad day," we would call it, knowing that we can usually choose the amount of another's sorrow and pain we want to rub up against with the same casualness that we would change television stations with the remote. For Ben, however, this is a typical day. He knows there are many more tragedies waiting to happen and, of course, we are never immune from bad days. To live our lives with courage, we must deny the patch of ice, the inattentive driver, the drunk, the one-in-a-million accident—indeed, our own inevitable deaths. But Ben is afforded no such luxury, and to be around him very long is to feel the fragility that is the human condition. During the past year, I have looked for any cracks in his armor, any flaws, and I have found not a bit of sarcasm or cynicism in Ben. He will tell you of his faith, which pulls him through. But what he so generously gives to others, day after day in the worst of conditions, is universal: A place to begin again. An orientation toward healing. Another chance.

On my way back to Pullman I notice that Huber's posted a message. It reads, "Pray for Jesse with the Bulldogs." And I do. I pray for Jesse.

SAVING
SCABLANDS

WHEAT IS A HEARTBREAKING $2.36 A BUSHEL, and farmers are in no mood to listen to any heartfelt testimonials from environmentalists. We are thrown up against each other in a stuffy public meeting room in Colfax, Washington. In front sit the members of the Whitman County Planning and Zoning Committee. They look at the crowd nervously. Usually no one goes to these meetings. But tonight, we are here to debate the fate of a section of desert in eastern Washington known as the Scablands.

At stake is a tumbled basalt rock landscape that would rival any of the more famous scenery in the Southwest. Parts of the Scablands could easily be a national park, similar to famous ones in Utah or Arizona. Here, though, the lands are mostly privately owned and posted with no trespassing signs. The fight is a common one in the West: development versus preservation. With grain and livestock prices low, cash-hungry farmers and ranchers would like to sell off some acres to residential developers by amending the county's tightfisted comprehensive plan. I am here to voice my opposition, but I can tell the decision is a fait accompli. Telling Western landowners what to do with their private property is akin to proposing socialism.

More than one rancher derisively refers to us as "those Pullman people," which refers to the presence in that town of Washington State University. The message is clear and not so far out: Too much education is bad and, coupled with too little physical labor, makes for odd tendencies, such as hugging trees and saving rocks.

"If you Pullman people want to help the rancher, you need to get this market coming around for us, get the cattle prices up so we can keep our ground!" The anger is stunning and frightening. Perhaps foolishly, I still feel heartened by so many opponents of this development scheme. There are certainly the college types cutting their teeth on public debate, but there are also teenagers, the elderly, and even more than one farmer.

My hands sweat as I approach the commissioners. I have not prepared a speech. Only after the long meeting will I remember geologist J. Harlan Bretz's 1928 quote etched in a modest memorial on top of Dry Falls, a lonely place where glacial floods once carved out an entire landscape of 3,000 square miles that stretches from Spokane south to the Snake River: "Ideas without precedent are generally looked upon with disfavor, and men are shocked when their conceptions of an orderly world are challenged."

Shocked is a good word to use when first seeing the Scablands. Within an hour east of this wheat town where we are meeting, columns of stacked basalt rise out of the earth like giant pieces of broken chalk; mesas and pinnacles abound, and long, bone-dry trenches—coulees—cast huge shadows across the desert. Few people live there. For now.

This geological wonder is a result of a series of cataclysmic floods that washed through the area more than 12,000 years ago during the Pleistocene epoch. A south-moving glacial ice dam blocked the Clark Fork River near present-day Sandpoint, Idaho, creating Glacial Lake Missoula. When the dam eventually burst, a watery hell broke loose. At its peak, 386 million cubic feet of water per second headed across northern Idaho and eastern Washington—ten times the combined flow of every river on earth. Bretz was the lone geologist who cracked the mystery of the Scablands in 1923, but not before he suffered decades of ridicule by skeptics.

Little of this geological wonder is public land. (Whitman County itself is 98 percent privately owned.) Perhaps the best exception is the Columbia National Wildlife Refuge, a small gem surrounded by the irrigated potato fields. Ducks, shorebirds, and thousands of migrating sandhill cranes and

Canada geese migrate through each year, stopping to rest on the refuge's pothole lakes and ponds.

Much of the floodwaters came down the Palouse River to slam against the wall of the Snake River breaks to form a massive gravel bar. It was at tiny Lyons Ferry State Park, on the banks of the warm, slack water of the Snake River, where I stood on a cliff looking up the Palouse River canyon to begin a week of following the floods. Cormorants, herons, coots, great-horned owls, and one rare mule deer with pan-sized ears shared my trip. On the opposite canyon walls I could easily distinguish "bathtub" rings, evidence of the numerous times the floodwater rose and sank. On that perfect morning it was hard to picture tract housing and gated communities.

I wish I could tell you that our eloquent testimony swayed the commissioners to vote against the zoning change. Or that a ten-to-one margin against the rezoning plan was enough. I tried to tell the story of the geological miracle and my week of following the floods. Tactfully, I attempted to say that what a landowner does with his acreage affects us all, and the peril of development to wildlife habitat. But all that came out was "You think it's worthless land, but it's not. Spend some time out there. You'll see."

But, of course, the landowners spend more time "out

there" than I ever will. And they don't believe the land is worthless. Far from it.

Eventually, and predictably, the amendment passed six votes to two. It's been a long, emotional night. On my way out, a rancher breaks away from a knot of other ranchers and farmers and confronts me.

"You probably don't like me," he says, his tone threatening. I can see his friends looking on, hoping for a heated argument, perhaps even a fistfight.

"No," I answer, "but I don't hate you. You just own more land than I do."

He shakes his head and strides away.

As I drive back to Pullman, I already know I will never see him again. I also don't ever want to attend another public meeting. Yet I know that's a foolish—and fleeting—conclusion to this emotional evening. I realize that both the rancher and I just shared in the messy activity of democracy. As fellow residents from different sides of town, so to speak, we both gave up a comfortable evening at home and, instead, hung our hearts out in public view because we care about this land we share. We probably at least agree on that.

As I drive home past the wheat and lentil fields between Colfax and Pullman, I remember the words of writer Jedediah Purdy, who at the wise age of twenty-four, wrote about public discussion in his book *For Common Things*: "Good lives argue for the adequacy of reality. They argue that our existence, with its limits, entanglements, necessary dependencies, and disappointments, is not to be escaped but to be contemplated more carefully and respectfully than it has been our recent practice to do so." Public action is organic work, often untidy, but possessing dignity.

By the time I pull into my driveway, I am already thinking of what I most wish I had said, standing at the front of that room: "I respect your views, and I hope you will respect mine. Now, where can we find common ground?"

RIVERS
NEVER DIE

O N A BALMY TUESDAY IN FEBRUARY, I stand on the old bridge by the Pullman Grange, watching dark chocolate-colored waves from the south fork of the Palouse River rapidly rise, when an elderly man approaches, wearing a tweed sports jacket. A camera hangs from his neck. He smiles at me. I have never seen him before.

Water barely grazes a 30-foot pipe that spans the river, carrying diesel fuel from large tanks on one side to gas pumps on the other. Another foot and the pipe will be underwater. Brave mallards float by squawking. The river moves at a speed that I sadly compare to the speed of computers. Nature now imitates technology. I really need to get out more.

The odor of soil is everywhere. I think of freshly dug red potatoes. "Earth apples," writer Ed Abbey called them. Instead of whitecaps there are brown caps. Dirt adheres to the roof of my mouth. I taste humus and the vague yeasty flavor of wheat. In about an hour that same soil will dump out into the Snake River with the rest of the silt.

Six days previous, 3 to 4 feet of snow blanketed this eastern Washington college town, closing schools and rural roads. The snow was unlike any seen in this part of the Palouse for quite some time. Not at all the usual coastal-influenced wet slush from the west side of the state we see most winters, this snow was dry with plenty of powder: the consistency of sand. Drifts rose in the wind. Ripples in the sides of great snowbanks froze, resembling geologic formations as if the canyons of southern Utah had just blown in. We could actually cross-country ski.

The man in the tweed jacket has something on his mind—something important to say about this flood. But first, he gets close to me, and we take in the scene together. He is at least seventy-five, with a face that has seen other floods. His eyes hold a silver gleam that he shines my way. He knows the intricate layers of what is happening at our feet, and now he wants to share.

At seven in the morning the day after the blizzard, as I waited for a commuter bus that never came, the snow clouds moved on to Montana and the Dakotas, and the temperature dove to 24 below. What little moisture there was in the air froze in a mirage of glorious ice crystals. On my walk that night I imagined the crunching sound of the dry snow was actually the crystals colliding against my body, like the tingle of a thousand small bells. A friend of mine in North Dakota says at 60 below it's remarkable how well your body adjusts. You discover new worlds within the extreme weather. Car exhaust and breath take center stage. You take chances with exposure, staying just a few minutes longer each time you venture outdoors.

Today, the temperature is a balmy 55 degrees. Waxwings cluster and sing overhead, fighting for position in the berry clusters of mountain ash trees. Juncos and finches drop from the clear blue sky. Patches of grass and the tips of daffodils emerge. This is hopeful weather, weather in which to lift one's face to the sun and imagine gardens.

My new friend edges nearer to me on the bridge, takes a deep whiff of the stinking water, and watches it disappear toward Colfax, to the confluence of the north fork of the Palouse River, and farther west into the basaltic Scablands of eastern Washington, scrubbed clean of topsoil by the glacial Missoula Flood 12,000 years ago. These ancient waters attained heights of several thousand feet and moved at speeds comparable to those of my Subaru. Most of the time the Palouse runs at under 300 cubic feet per second (cfs). By the end of the day it will top 4,000 cfs. It demands our attention. The heart of the river is beating once again, but not everyone is pleased.

Earlier, Pullman High School students were dismissed for the day to help sandbag the downtown businesses whose buildings backed up against the river. A narrow alley behind those buildings is now beneath 4 feet of water. The river splashed against the back walls of White's Drugs, Swilley's restaurant, Ken Vogel's clothing store, First National Bank, and Budget Tapes and Records. It reminded me of pictures I had seen of canals in Venice, Italy. The transformed downtown was as disorienting as the change in temperature.

At Safeway the bottled water sold out, even the expensive French brands. The hilltop site of the new multimillion-dollar Living Faith Fellowship Church had fresh erosion cracks that revealed exposed sections of the recently poured asphalt parking lot. Three Spokane television station satellite trucks hovered at the edges of the flood like vultures on a death watch, waiting for the first drowning, the first casualty of "nature's fury."

But nothing was happening except the river rising, and a makeshift espresso stand was doing a whale of a business with the high school kids. On the news that night I watched the reporters stand on the bridges for their live feeds with nothing much to report, improvising with weather updates and school closures. The trucks pulled out the next day for more fertile disaster ground downriver. The *Spokesman Review* wrote of "a mean, muddy river." The governor declared our county—Whitman—and many surrounding counties, official disaster areas.

Local reports started trickling in: The highway into the town of Palouse was closed, its downtown completely under water, including a stately art deco bridge; in Albion, the water system was contaminated, and the highway patrol was issuing tickets to anyone caught trying to drive the main highway out of town; 20,000 out of the 75,000 acres of winter wheat planted in Columbia County had been destroyed; nervous Colfax residents had disobeyed their fire chief and gathered on the levee to sandbag; across the border in Moscow, Idaho, the university had closed. Pullman, miraculously, had been spared any widespread damage.

In fact, the atmosphere in downtown Pullman was a mix of the festive and the apocalyptic. Families and their children—some in strollers, with dogs tied behind—casually hiked the railroad trestle along the river while more sandbags were filled and piled high. "Now, what river is this?" some asked. Hoses snaked along the sidewalks in an attempt to pump water from the basements of businesses right back into the river. Police and firefighters sealed off certain sections with yellow crime tape. Red and amber lights flashed and reflected off storefronts.

Many people in Pullman don't realize they have a river running through it. In this eastern Washington portion of the Columbia Plain, the Palouse River drains most of the country north of the Snake River. Yet the river usually resembles an insignificant creek, and a polluted one at that, tainted by the runoff from agricultural pesticides and fertilizers. When Wendell Berry visited this area, he said it looked as if the steep fields were farmed to the point of desperation. He was remarking on the worst of the wheat and pea fields that grow right up to the edge of roads without any vegetative cover for pheasants or birds. The blue bunch grass and Idaho fescue—native perennial grasses of the Palouse—are long gone, first to grazing by cattle and sheep, who turned those grasses into annuals, then to the plow, which finished them off. Richard Manning, in his book *Grassland*, writes of annual loss of topsoil to wind erosion here at "one hundred tons per acre, or an inch of topsoil removed to the wind every 1.6 years." If you take in account these warm thaws and January chinook winds, that rate must be even higher.

In spite of farming pressures, though, the river somehow remains alive, this body of moving water that partly begins in the Hoo Doo Mountains of neighboring Idaho and empties out via the 300-foot Palouse Falls through wild, inaccessible canyons into what some locals call Snake Lake, a river emasculated by four redundant dams in its lower reaches and another dozen or so upriver in Idaho. My wife and I make a habit of following stretches of the Palouse River every summer when the roads dry out to honor its presence, to acknowledge a sense of riverness. This is our home, no matter how many scars, and we believe in this river.

Parts of the river are spectacular, especially parts inaccessible to vehicles or agriculture. Herons are not an uncommon sight, also kingfishers, ducks, owls, and hawks. A friend's son fishes different pools for pan-sized trout, but he won't reveal where. Bone-colored basalt cliffs line a stretch near the settlement of Elberton, and untouched ponderosa pines grow directly out of those rocks. I have experienced that lonely, wilderness feeling walking to the Middle Falls, the same enhanced awareness I have felt in "official" wilderness areas. A small island sits not far from Colfax, a complex knot of trees, plants, and bushes, untouched by development and as pretty a piece of riparian area as I have ever seen in the West. The Palouse River is not dead.

The man on the bridge with the camera is finally ready to talk to me. "Do you know 'The Rime of the Ancient Mariner'?" he asks. Before I can answer that I have heard of it, sort of, he looks out at the river, closes his eyes, and begins: "Water, water, every where, / And all the boards did shrink; / Water, water, every where, / Nor any drop to drink. . . ." When he finishes, we look at the river for a long time, watching it spill its banks, reaching for the streets.

A COMMUNITY
OF BOOKS

I N THE LAST FEW YEARS, *COMMUNITY* HAS EMERGED
as the newest environmental word du jour. We have lost all
sense of community, and without it we are doomed to a life of
the impersonal, writers solemnly tell us. Unless we take action
now, we will soon be reduced to cable-watching automatons
imprisoned in our homes, withering away in fear and depres-
sion, drinking the wrong kind of chardonnay, and wearing too
much polyester.

As the newest doom-and-gloom set grimly press on at
seminars with titles like "Representing Place: A Conference
on Literature, Language, and the Arts," the speakers, who
are making a fast buck on the lecture circuit from all this
doomsday talk, give us their "vision" for a happy, improved
world:

Independent bookstores will blossom along with movie
houses that feature low-budget art films that only a hundred
people in the world understand. Interspersed will be fertile
organic community gardens, weed-free green spaces with

paths for reckless mountain bikers and in-line skaters, farmer's markets and food co-ops brimming with only healthy food and the occasional chocolate bar. Most patrons will eat crisp, organic Macintosh apples that cost $1.75 per pound and sip $3.00 coffees. Labrador retrievers with red kerchiefs tied around their necks will lie in the sun: unattended and unleashed, of course. Everyone will be an environmentalist and will agree on just exactly what that term means. The speakers envision downtown Main Street awash with coffee hangouts, Thai restaurants, dependable public transportation, ample and free parking, and, surprise!, people just like them.

Now, I admit green belts are lovely, even though in the dry West it takes gallons of precious, aquifer-sucking water, exotic lawn grasses, pesticides, and nonnative plants to pull it off. Believe it or not, community has always been strong in the West and remains so today.

One of my many jobs while living in the West was that of an Idaho State Library Scholar, a fancy term for someone who risks his life on icy roads each winter to drive to tiny Idaho towns to discuss books with small audiences of dedicated readers. The program is called "Let's Talk About It." The books follow a theme: "Idaho: Tough Paradise," "Not for Children Only," and "Women's Lives" are just a few of these excellent topics. We gathered in one-room libraries, senior centers, and sometimes in the meeting rooms of motels. Cookies, percolated coffee, and homemade sweets are served. Populations in the towns I regularly visited are sometimes as small as 156 (Elk River), but no larger than 3,228 (Grangeville). I've been to Peck, Orofino, Bovill, Bonners Ferry, and many others.

Books in the programs serve as springboards into issues that truly affect communities. And trust me on this one: No one is discussing Thai restaurants or bike paths.

In Wallace we dissected Leslie Silko's *Ceremony*, then took on the current state of affairs of mining. People shared the personal devastation the downturn in silver mining had on their families. The idleness in the mines at that time was destroying good, hardworking men, with the women and children caught in the swift economic current, too.

In Grangeville, after discussing Russell Baker's *Growing Up*, I heard sad stories about newcomers who move in and decline to participate in the town's activities. "I had one man refuse to come to an important meeting," a woman said. "He told me he moved here to get away from all of that stuff."

My favorite stop was the logging town of Pierce, a tight-knit community of 617 high above the Clearwater River in north central Idaho on the edge of what should be wilderness, but remains perilously unprotected and contentiously fought over. Snow lingers well into summer, and to reach

Pierce is to drive the Greer Grade up out of the river through thick fog and the usual horrific patches of cracked asphalt Idaho calls roads.

From the outside, Pierce doesn't look like much: a few combination bar-restaurant-day care centers, and a disjointed menagerie of modest houses and trailers. Sidewalks are nonexistent, and logging trucks park on the front lawns. Dogs roam free, but there are no green belts. Nothing about this place is glamorous, and there is no danger of Pierce becoming the next Ketchum or Vail. It's just a place where people live community each and every day, like a reflex.

Pierce's library patrons have survived the bust and boom of the timber industry and currently are not faring well. You might expect them to be bitter, but their kindness, intelligence, and wisdom are qualities that are wise to listen to and to emulate.

"People say we don't love the land, but they're wrong. We know this country better than the environmentalists," one woman told me. "But has anyone bothered to ask us our opinions?" Others join in with beautiful descriptions of recently spotted wildlife and a reverence for life.

"We have a great community in Pierce," another woman says, and every head in the library nods in agreement. "We look after each other up here. I wouldn't live anywhere else."

ACROSS THE CHECKERBOARD WITH DWIGHT

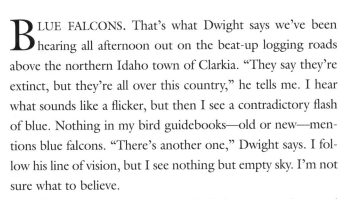

BLUE FALCONS. That's what Dwight says we've been hearing all afternoon out on the beat-up logging roads above the northern Idaho town of Clarkia. "They say they're extinct, but they're all over this country," he tells me. I hear what sounds like a flicker, but then I see a contradictory flash of blue. Nothing in my bird guidebooks—old or new—mentions blue falcons. "There's another one," Dwight says. I follow his line of vision, but I see nothing but empty sky. I'm not sure what to believe.

This country is a giant bowl of clear-cuts and second growth, and soon-to-be third growth, the old growth of cedar and white pine replaced by nursery-grown hemlock. Also present is a botanical stew of dying native plants and aggressive, exotic forest invaders, like meadow and orange hawkweed, a species that can produce 3,200 plants per square yard. Everywhere in various stages of decay are what Dwight calls "black pine," a spindly little tree that he says was planted by Roosevelt's Civilian Conservation Corps to combat erosion. "They weren't supposed to live this long," Dwight grumbles, as if their death couldn't come too soon. Any biological diversity that once existed has been replaced with moonscapes and slash piles the size of stadiums. *Panoramic* is an oddly appropriate word to describe the clear-cuts we drive through. So complete and final. And quiet. In just a decade Idaho has lost one million roadless acres, or 11.4 acres per hour.

Sadly, I am no longer shocked by the devastation. Maybe this is destruction fatigue. After twenty-five years out West, my heart has been broken so many times that I've built up an immunity. It's a desperate and mostly failed attempt at self-protection. When did I cross over? When did I stop believing in the permanence of landscape? Maybe it was the stand of redwoods that disappeared overnight near Blue Lake, California, or the four-lane, paved road punched in through the old-growth country of the high Siskyous. Maybe it was in Colorado when the Animas River turned the color of mercury after a mine's tailings pond broke and dumped its poisons into the waters. Maybe it was after a tractor trailer of chemicals crashed into the Little Salmon River and killed every single fish. Whatever it is, I am not proud of my reaction today. I should be outraged, but instead I am worn out.

Dwight is a different story. At sixty-eight, Dwight should by all rights be dead from all the dangerous woods work he's done, or at least retired, and I guess he is from logging, road building, and all other forms of body-breaking labor that are common up here in the Idaho mountains. Skinny as a snow pole, his body a bag of protruding bones, Dwight hardly has a waist to hang his jeans on. He breathes from an inhaler every couple of hours. He has colitis, congestive heart failure, and 20 percent heart efficiency, which almost led to his death this past spring when he got pneumonia. He looks ten years older than he actually is, but he hears and sees perfectly and knows all the plants and trees and subtle contours within a hundred miles. Speaking of snow poles: "You know Jim, don't you?" Dwight asks. "One winter he stole a bunch of these snow poles. Good wood. But the Department of Transportation guys finally caught him in the spring when he used the poles for his garden fence."

Dwight always has some scheme in the works, like a warehouse-load of older model car and truck parts he traded a .30 gauge shotgun for—and that are sitting in his Elk River shop.

It's a good thing, too, about the automotive parts, because the starter on this pickup truck that Dwight has me, my wife, Jan, his wife, Carol, and their black poodle, Lady, cramped into is quickly deteriorating. Every time he turns the key he expends another act of faith. The windshield's shattered, too, and with each bump the crack expands like a spider's web. We're 30 or so miles from any help, another 40 from a good auto repair shop, and 150 from the nearest emergency room. But Dwight has a spare starter under the seat, along with a loaded .357, and all kinds of stuff I can feel rolling underneath my butt every time he hits one of those Forest Service–dug Kelly humps—put in, Dwight complains, to keep the public out. This complaint leads to a lecture on the different philosophies of two Forest Service district supervisors: The district ranger in the St. Joe National Forest keeps the roads maintained because he wants people to enjoy the forest; the district ranger in the Clearwater National Forest is a mean so-and-so who wants to keep the taxpayers down below on the paved roads.

For no good reason, I have complete faith in Dwight's ability to navigate us safely through this maze of new and neglected skid roads. Maybe because he's so well prepared. Jacks, thermoses, come-alongs, chains, ropes, a shovel, a cooler, spare bullets, standard and metric wrenches all jostle around in the bed of the pickup. "Hold onto Lady's leg so she won't fall out," Carol tells me, as we all bounce up and down like kids on a trampoline.

Storytelling keeps Dwight's mind in motion, and driving around this country ensures that his emotions stay sharp. "I was riding my three-wheeler down a road just the other day when here comes a Forest Service truck. This ranger, a young guy, said, 'Can't you read?' I said, 'Yes.' 'Then why are you driving on this road?' I said, 'Because my taxes helped pay for this gravel, and I'm just using up my share.' He said, 'Don't get smart with me. I'll have you arrested. And what gives you the authority to drive on this road?' I reach down and pull out my .357 and answer, 'This gives me the authority.' Well, the guy drives off real fast, and I figure the sheriff is going to be waiting for me at my house when I get back to town. But he isn't."

Three days later, Dwight is on the same closed road, and he meets the same guy in the truck. "This time he didn't even slow down or look at me," Dwight says.

I've heard this story before, from other people, on a similar theme: Native, hardworking Idahoan stands up to a cocky, disrespectful U.S. Forest Service employee, or some other federal authority figure bent on denying property and gun rights, who, when faced with the great western equalizer—a loaded gun—backs down and slinks away. In this part of Idaho, it's hard to find people who are not suspicious of anyone in a uniform.

Just after Dwight tells his story, he pulls the pickup over to the side of the road, jumps out, and, with an agility he shouldn't have, clambers up into a second-growth mess. He comes back with a bouquet of huckleberry plants torn out at the roots. "The Forest Service says this is illegal. I could get a fine for pulling off these branches. But they will allow 4,000 sheep to graze up here and eat everything down to the ground. Now, is that fair?" He has a point. He usually does. We stand around the bed of the pickup, delicately relieving the branches of the tiny berries, while he disappears to bring back armful upon armful of illegal plants.

We will climb the same steep hills from where the steam engines used to winch millions of board feet up the top of a hill known as The Incline in the early part of last century to waiting narrow-gauge trains. We will only get out of the truck to eat lunch, drink coffee from Dwight's battered thermos, pee, and pick huckleberries.

This trip was Dwight's idea—a birthday present to Jan—to show her how the roads connect up here and to teach us some of the history of how this country was opened up. She's known Dwight for more than a decade and constantly teases him, which he visibly enjoys. "Now, Dwight, is there any difference between a good story and a lie?" Most of Dwight's stories are true, or at least close enough to truth for telling, and all of them good ones. I don't know what to believe. "There's not a woman in Elk River over the age of sixty-five who wasn't a whore once," he declares at one point. Carol quickly reminds us that she is not quite sixty.

Dwight and Carol have been together forty-four years and married for forty-one. They belong to the Seventh-Day Adventist Church. By the age of twenty, Carol had borne four children. Then she had another. They fed their children a diet of poached deer and elk that Dwight smuggled in the bottom of gasoline fuel drums past the Forest Service checkpoint at Clarkia. "They knew I was getting game, but they couldn't figure it out," he says.

Dwight has worked in the woods all his life, except for a stint in the Merchant Marines and four years serving in the Korean War after lying about his age—fifteen at the time. He built and maintained roads up and down this country, logged for himself and others, and worked for the Forest Service at a time when he says it was still an honorable profession. He can tear down and fix anything.

Carol cans all their food, as she's done for four decades. This time of year—August and early September—she picks and sells huckleberries. Twenty dollars a gallon: washed and cleaned. Because the berries are unusually small this year, it takes her an hour to pick a quart. Her labor comes to $5.00

an hour. Carol does a lot of trading—huckleberries for corn, huckleberries to pay for the year's rent for Dwight's shop, huckleberries for quilt scraps—she cleans houses, and for a modest fee she transports folks in Elk River to the hospitals in Lewiston and Moscow.

Dwight hates water. Instead, he prefers coffee and Pepsi. He used to drink a half gallon of Canadian Mist a day. On his fiftieth birthday he drank his usual ration plus another fifth his boss gave him, then a fresh fifth of vodka at a friend's house. His buddies were all taking bets to see when Dwight would keel over. At 3:00 A.M. he was still drinking the vodka and telling stories. His companions had passed out.

"But that's not why I stopped drinking," he says. "I quit because I lost a whole week of my life, and I still don't know what I did that week. I had a job as a welder, and they say I went to work and did my job. But I don't remember it." The next week Dwight came home and said to Carol, "That's it. I quit."

He still has a drink now and then, Carol gently reminds him, like last year at the Lewiston rodeo. He quit smoking cigarettes last year, a habit he began at the age of ten. Wasn't hard, he boasts: "I say if you're going to do something, just do it."

At lunch, while our wives are off talking, Dwight calls me over to the truck and shows me the .357 handgun. Then he reaches in his pocket and digs out four of his special "people bullets" that will "tear a big hole in a man. You never know what you'll find up here." He slips me the pistol, and for the first time in my life I hold a gun. It feels good, like a well-made tool. My initial impulse is to shoot it randomly into the woods, but I hand it back to Dwight.

"When did you fire this last?" I ask.

"Yesterday, at a rock 25 yards away."

"Did you hit it?"

"You bet."

I BROUGHT A CLEARWATER NATIONAL FOREST and Palouse Ranger District of the St. Joe National Forest map to keep up with Dwight, but within an hour into the trip we have driven off the map. The map is useless anyway. In addition to its unwieldy size—4 feet by 4 feet—and the dozens of folds that are hard to negotiate with Lady tap dancing on my thighs with her sharp claws, there are too many colors. There are thirteen, many in earth shades of red and clay and brown, and each color represents a landowner. When I spread the map out, it looks like those early maps of Africa after the European powers carved it up. For a state like Idaho that complains about all the federal non-tax-paying lands—more than 70 percent of the state is federally owned—a map like this one shows a rather different version. Five of the owners are timber companies: Champion International, SAW Forest Products, Potlatch Corporation, Plum Creek Timber Co., Inc., and Bennett Tree Farms Inc. One color will run into another, and sometimes a square-mile square will have three or four colors competing for ownership. Even when the dominant color of the squares is dark green, signifying public lands, a patchwork of Plum Creek Timber Co. Inc., pink, intrudes.

The reason for the checkerboard appearance of this map, and most Forest Service maps in the West, is because of an act of Congress. The 1864 Northern Pacific Railroad Land Grant is perhaps the one document most responsible for the presence of private timber company holdings in America's public lands. In the 1995 book *Railroads and Clearcuts*, by Derrick Jensen and George Draffan, the authors write, "In 1864, during the Civil War, the United States Congress created the Northern Pacific Railroad Company and empowered it to construct a rail line from Lake Superior to Puget Sound. To aid in the construction and maintenance of the railroad, Congress conditionally granted Northern Pacific nearly 40 million acres of land." At the time, this was 2 percent of the entire forty-eight states, almost the equivalent in area of present-day Washington State. The amount of right-of-way in the grant was not large, 200 feet on either side of the proposed tracks, and some ground for stations.

The largest portion of the grant was for construction and maintenance of the rail system: a band 40 miles wide through the states of Wisconsin, Minnesota, and Oregon; 80 miles wide through the territories of North Dakota, Montana, Idaho, and Washington. Land was granted in alternating square miles, and, as Jensen and Draffan write, "a 'checkerboard' pattern of ownership was created that is still visible on maps and landscapes of many Pacific Northwest forests."

Most of the day Dwight leads us through lands owned by one of the principal beneficiaries of the 1864 Northern Pacific Railroad Land Grant Act, Potlatch Corporation. We also pass briefly through Bureau of Land Management property at Hobo Pass, as well as a few miles of area labeled on the map in green as "Adjacent National Forest Lands," which looks a lot like the well-used Potlatch land. Millions of board feet have been harvested from these "working forests."

"IT MUST HAVE QUITE A FEAT to build those donkey steam engine railroads up these steep Idaho hills to get at all these trees," I say as we inch along, sheer drop-offs out my window.

"It took a lot of dead men and a lot of will power," Dwight whispers. "The woods is the great killer of men." We pause along an abandoned watering stop for trains. Dwight points at a hill. "Imagine hauling a 30-pound saw, gallon can of gasoline and oil, a saw kit, ax and hatchet and wedges, a maul, and your lunch pail up that bank in two feet of snow," he says solemnly. "Then you'll understand why there were so many drunken lumberjacks." We sit in the cab for awhile with the engine idling and no one speaking; incredibly, not even Dwight, who continues to stare up the hillside as if expecting the ghosts of broken loggers to come marching slowly down toward us, the sun glaring off their steel helmets and suspenders.

Dwight can't maintain the silence for long and soon launches into another story. When no one let the water out of the dam at the Elk Creek pond in April and Dwight's shop, with all those car parts, was flooded with spring runoff, he called the Idaho Department of Parks and Recreation and warned that if they didn't start letting some water out, he was going to dynamite the dam, and then they could figure out how to fix it. They let the water out. "Next spring, if they don't let the water out, I'm going down there with a D-7 Cat," he says.

The real reason his shop was flooded was because a town official, who has a key to the dam's lock, hates Dwight. This dates to an incident years ago when they were logging together. The guy was a loader at the time, and Dwight was a logging truck driver. Each time his adversary loaded logs on Dwight's truck, he would tear off (purposely, Dwight maintains) the truck's mirrors.

"Finally, I says to him, 'If you don't stop hitting my mirrors, I'm coming up there with my ax, and we'll straighten it out.' He laughs and takes some logs and tears my mirror off. I jumped into that cab with my ax, and he took off and ran down the road. The big boss comes up and says, 'What's going on up here?' I tell him, and he orders the guy to pay for my mirror, or he'll write him a pink slip on the spot. The guy pays for the mirror, and we never had any more trouble." Until he got the key to the dam.

We drive on, and Dwight becomes confused by all the new roads. "You have to come out here every couple of months because everything changes all the time," he grumbles, dodging another newly washed out portion of a logging road.

LITTLE WONDER DWIGHT IS CONFUSED. The Clearwater National Forest has 4,558 miles of roads within its borders. To the north, in the Panhandle National Forest, are 8,312 miles of roads, or 10 miles of roads for every square mile of land, the highest density of roads of any national forest in the United States. Both figures are probably low. If one factored in "jammer roads," abandoned skid roads built in the 1950s and 1960s, the original figures might double. More than 440,000 miles of roads jigsaw through our public forests, or roughly ten times the entire U.S. interstate system. You could drive the quarter of a million miles to the moon and still have plenty of road left over.

DWIGHT FINDS HIS WAY AROUND BY SEARCHING for landmarks: Freezeout Ridge, Cornwall Peak, Grandmother Mountain and Grandfather Mountain, Elk Butte, Orphan Peak, and a new cell phone dish on the top of a nameless hill. But how can he still identify them when they are bare of trees? The lack of birds, deer, squirrels, and people is eerie.

We end our eight-hour day of driving at a cafe in Fernwood, Idaho. Dwight calls Fernwood "Funnywood." In the

men's room are two posters of women in bikinis, one strad-
dling a Harley, the other, right above the toilet, standing on
a beach, holding a wet beer bottle with droplets of water
dripping down her tight abdomen. Radio news reports are
filtering in that Princess Diana has been involved in a single
car crash in Paris, but that she survived. No one pays any
attention. In this isolated part of America, the idea of France
is equivalent to the idea of Mars.

This will be our last trip together. In a year Dwight will
be housebound, hooked up to a bottle of oxygen. The huckleberries will be even smaller and less abundant. I will travel
very little into the mountains in the coming year, too. I have
excuses, plenty of them: my daughter's last year of high
school; a commitment to drive less and use fewer resources;
an undependable car; and a lack of time. Closer to the truth
is that I want to preserve the image of wilderness that I first
saw when I came out West twenty-five years ago. What we
witnessed today is too much truth. Miles upon miles of
clear-cuts with no end in sight. Silt-choked streams and
rivers in muddy ruin. No animals or birds. An emptiness
of landscape and still an insatiable consumption. We are
never full.

Jan, who knows Dwight well, tells me he feels the weight
of loss, too. After all, he's worked out here all his life. Many

of his sentences begin, "I remember when . . ." Dwight will see the destruction through to the end. He can't turn away. I can come and go from these mountains as I please. I am hardly privileged, though, or better than Dwight because I love grizzlies, wolves, and trees. Dwight loves them, too, but on a more intimate level. He paid for his love with his health. I sign petitions and write letters.

Dwight had his favorite groves, but only a handful remain, like the stand of cedars and alder where we ate lunch. After hours of driving in deforested areas that were unnaturally hot, the tiny forest was a throwback: cool and shaded, and filled with birdsong and native plant. Somewhere in the distance we could hear water running. Dwight seemed at his happiest during lunch, commenting, "When you spend a day up here in the woods, you just know there is a creator."

I often think of Dwight's comment about a creator, especially when I am walking through a forest. For all the recent writings about nature I cannot recall a more eloquent statement. Now when I mourn the wildness we have lost, I cannot separate Dwight from that loss.

At the cafe, while we drink the worst coffee I have ever had, I tell Dwight that I once drove all the way to Montana without hitting pavement. He laughs. "Heck, I can drive to

Canada without touching pavement. Have to cross a couple of highways, though." Then he tells me how he would do it: Avoid the lakes, stay to the east of Sandpoint, drop down into Libby, follow the Yaak River north, and you can cross the border at any number of places. No checkpoints, too, he says with a smile, like he's done this a hundred times. And I believe him, every word.

RECOMMITMENT

NINE BARK, OCEAN SPRAY, AND FAT SNOWBERRIES greet Jan and me at the entrance to the trail at the northwest flank of Kamiak Butte in eastern Washington. It's our first wedding anniversary, and it's love and recommitment that draw us here this October afternoon.

Dozens of wildflowers we marveled at in the open, sensual days of late April are long gone: Dwarf waterleaf. Mountain bluebell. Fairy slipper. Fawn lily. Starflower. Shooting star. Larkspur. Arrow leaf balsam root. Yellow bells. Forget-me-nots. Trillium. Blue-eyed grass.

Now only the stubborn mountain aster and the hearty Indian paintbrush survive these first days of frost. The trail is slick, and the roots of Douglas fir and ponderosa pine lie exposed like strong, tan arms pushing through the duff. Everywhere I can sense a shift in light toward the dim end of the spectrum.

As FAMILIAR AS THIS TRAIL IS, my mind is on other, more exotic landscapes we took in during a recent weeklong camping trip through the belly of Idaho. I'm not quite home yet. After twelve years of living here, I'm not convinced that I'm living in the right place. On this day of love, I want to be won over again, courted and sparked. I want some flirtation.

How easy it is to love jagged mountains and hot springs, mystical deserts and rushing white rivers. How simple to drive and hike and put up the tent at the end of a day of motion and exploration. And how hard sometimes it is to come back home.

My head is soggy with self-perceived images of pristine, unspoiled wildness and what Carl Anthony, the director of Earth Island, calls "the mystique of whiteness." For wilderness is really more a state of mind than reality. Here's a sample of what we saw during that September trip: a flotilla of mergansers bobbing and dipping down the narrow passage of the Salmon River at Sunbeam; clusters of shy preening western white pelicans, surrounded by hundreds of diving grebes at Cascade Reservoir.

A single, 4-foot gopher snake in search of dinner at Bruneau Dunes.

A herd of antelope framed at the base of Mount Borah just beyond the 21-mile 1983 earthquake scarp that runs along the western slope of the Lost River Range.

A recurring bumper sticker in Challis: "Environmentalists: Welcome to Salmon. We haven't had a hanging since 1964."

Limber pines growing out of whispers of soil blown between the lava, and Clark's nutcrackers at Craters of the Moon. An entire landscape in transition.

A cattle drive in the middle of Highway 93, with a lone buckaroo dressed the part except for wraparound Oakley sunglasses and a cellular phone sticking out of his leather vest.

Hiking at dusk over a slab of granite at the City of Rocks, we came upon 1,000 migrating turkey vultures roosting in an aspen grove. Long leathery necks and red skull caps turned in our direction as if to say: "We hope you die soon." Below, in the wide empty valley, the names of California Trail pioneers are eternally preserved in axle grease on a rock face.

Big, lonely, romantic country, all of it. Seductive, too, and that's the tricky part. Passing through, the pleasure is purely aesthetic. Skin deep, like admiring a fine thoroughbred horse. As much as I can picture myself in the middle of these flashy scenes, the truth is, I could never live in tiny

Idaho towns like Arco, Challis, Burley, or Almo. I've already given my heart away.

JUST PAST THE BRIDGE, deep in the north-facing grand firs, Jan's voice breaks through: "It's moving again. It's always moving." She is looking at Steptoe Butte, which began to our right and has now jumped behind us. Steptoe, that shifty pyramid, topped with a healthy layer of Mount St. Helens ash, always floats up on the horizon at some odd angle without warning. Sometimes just a tip as you're driving through the wheat, and sometimes the full triangle, catching light and dispensing shadow. Twin granite partner of Kamiak, separated in height by only 37 feet. It's not 12,662-foot Mount Borah, the tallest peak in Idaho. Not snow-capped. Not perfect. And not pretty to some who base their standard of beauty on the majestic.

Now we are walking straight up the steepest part of Kamiak, hearts beating savagely against gravity's weight. I picture my own heart attempting to break open through bone and skin, breaking through to the land's core. I imagine flowing with the river, beginning at Laird Park out of the Hoodoos, crossing Highway 95 south the Potlatch turnoff, running past the basalt cliffs at Elberton and joining forks at Colfax, passing the abandoned flour mill at Winona and the tidy MacGregor company town of Hooper, moving across the Scablands, raking off topsoil as we plunge over Palouse Falls to empty at Lyons Ferry at the Snake River. These are hardly flashy waters like the Salmon or the Payette. They are full of intervention and silt and god knows what. This is not wilderness, but something to improve on, something like the human spirit.

Senegalese conservationist Baba Dioum says, "In the end, we will conserve only what we love, we will love only what we understand, and we will understand only what we are taught." After a decade of living in the middle of wheat, I'm only just now beginning to understand this land.

At the top of the Butte, where the trees give way to one of the last stretches of bunchgrass prairie in the Palouse, we rest and take in the view to the south. I look out at the fissures, cracks, and wrinkles, and I think of my own life's history down below: discovery, divorce, separation, resurrection, renewal, fatherhood. Love. Land. The two are inseparable. The late nature writer Edward Abbey wrote, "THIS IS WHAT YOU SHALL DO: Love the earth and the sun and the animals. Stand up for the stupid and the crazy." I like to believe he was inclusive and meant that we should love our own internal landscape of scars, and the beauty that in our most human, our most humane moments, we are capable of creating. For nature is not separate from us, like those idealized paintings from the nineteenth century that showed the American continent empty, bright, and celestial. We have a landscape inside of us every bit as wild and beautiful as a forest of cedar; and how we feel about ourselves will have more to do with preserving the health and balance of ecosystems than signing a check to an organization or even, I will offer, involvement in our political system.

How quickly political boundaries dissolve and land comes together up here on Kamiak. Looking down past Moscow and Pullman, I see the canyon breaks above Lewiston, with a gap in the center that holds the confluence of the Clearwater and Snake rivers; above the rivers' shores is the bump at Field Spring State Park, and slightly west of that the Blue Mountains and the Tucannon country of northeastern Oregon. If the sky was perfectly clear, the faint outline of the Seven Devils Mountains would be visible—more than 150 miles to the south.

Up here we orient ourselves to the landscape. And if we let down our guard, let our hearts break open, and begin to offer words to a new definition of wilderness, we can also orient our very lives in the fields and forests, towns and streams of the Palouse. Love. Land.

In the essay "Winter Solstice at Moab Slough," Terry Tempest Williams asks, "What kind of impoverishment is this to withhold emotion, to restrain our passionate nature in the face of a generous life just to appease our fears? . . . Our lack of intimacy with each other is in direct proportion to our lack of intimacy with the land. We have taken our love inside and abandoned the wild."

Jan takes my hand. I pull her in close, look into her brown eyes that have swallowed stars, and whisper, "Happy anniversary."

"Happy anniversary to you, too. Thank you for sharing your life with me."

The wind begins to lift off the fields and drift up the hill. There's a distinct chill in the air. Time to put up storm windows. Time to pick the dozens of green tomatoes, roll them out on the windowsill, and hope for the best. Turn the compost. Shake out the quilts. Trim the iris patch, fill the flower beds with leaves. Time to make rice and chili, and apple pies. It's autumn. Time to come down off the mountain. Time to come back down to earth.

LEAVING
THE WEST

THE FIRST TIME I HEAR THE VOICE is in the fall, when the larch trees have just begun to change color. I'm driving out of Washington's Blue Mountains along Cloverland Road, just above the Snake River. Cloverland is a series of hairpin turns and S curves bordered by a sheer drop into a canyon full of snakes, sage, and yellow star thistle. My fifteen-year-old, oil-leaking Subaru leans toward the drop-off, and, like a whisper, I hear this command:

Go straight.

My arms stiffen, and I turn the wheel too slowly going into the sharp turns. My brake foot is sluggish. I'm having trouble coordinating the clutch and the gas pedal. Far below, at the bottom of the canyon, the cattle look like dots. I wouldn't be found for a week.

Give in.

My fingers are purple and sticky from picking huckleberries. It's the second bad growing season in a row, and all I have to show for an afternoon's work is one sorry baggie full of berries, barely enough for my wife, Jan, to eke out a batch of muffins. A friend, Jake, sits quietly in the passenger seat, oblivious to how close he is to death.

Jake lives on $300 a month, doesn't own a television, a phone, or a car (a bicycle is his only mode of transportation), and shops exclusively at Goodwill. When he invited us over for Thanksgiving dinner once, we had to bring our own dishes and chairs. When Jake was a child, he was often in his room stacking pennies. When he visits his sister in New Orleans, he takes the Greyhound: $59, round trip. Reading on the bus makes him nauseous, so he stares out the window for four days. What he thinks about, I have no idea.

Go ahead. See what it's like to fly.

I finally recognize the voice; it's my own, only an octave lower.

I manage to keep the car on the road, mostly because I like Jake and don't want to kill him by driving this hunk of junk off a basalt cliff and onto a pregnant heifer hundreds of feet below. Finally, we make it to the bottom of the grade, and the voices cease. Jake yawns and asks where we are. "On level ground," I tell him.

Every four or five years, Jake moves to a new location. Each new place of residence must meet his strict requirements: It must be a college town west of the Great Divide, and the university must have an Olympic-size pool where Jake can swim laps for free. (Also, Jake can shower and shave at the pool, and thus turn off the hot-water heater at home.) The libraries must be well stocked. The student union must provide phones where he can make free local calls and televisions where he can watch his favorite football team, the Broncos. In the last ten years, Jake has lived in Pocatello, Idaho; Flagstaff, Arizona; and Fort Collins, Colorado. He is fifty-two years old, as thin as a Q-Tip, and as stubborn as the NRA.

To me, the most incredible thing of all about Jake's lifestyle is that he neither has nor wants a girlfriend. I try not to ask him too many questions, but eventually I have to ask him about this. The summer following that car rider, around a campfire in the Bitterroot Mountains, I say: "How do you do it, Jake? How have you managed to escape women?"

He looks across the flames and without pausing says, "They're too damn expensive! If I get involved with a woman, she'll want us to have a car, and then I'll have to get my own car. Then suddenly we've got two cars and a phone that won't quit ringing, and she'll probably already have children, and . . ." His voice trails off. "I was interested in a woman in Boulder, but the first time I invited her over for dinner, she saw I didn't have any wine and ran out to the nearest liquor store and bought *three* bottles. I knew then it wasn't going to work out."

Based on my relationship track record, I probably would have insisted on paying for the wine. My mantra is "Please don't be mad at me. I'll change; I promise. More wine?" Women scare the daylights out of me, even when they're 5 feet tall and weigh 100 pounds. Once, a woman tried to bill me for her counseling after we broke up.

So I look at Jake and think, *You're my hero, man.* I hold him in the same esteem as I do the lone sockeye salmon that made it to Idaho's Redfish Lake this year, bobbing and weaving through the dozen dams or so along the Columbia and Snake rivers, finally arriving in the Sawtooths in a horrible state, only to spawn and die. Jake would make it through; I'd get chewed up in the turbines at the first dam.

Jake places another stick on the fire. "Does Jan still want to move back to Illinois to be near her folks?" he asks.

"Yes," I say. "She's going no matter what. She says I'm welcome to join her."

Her father has skin cancer and is undergoing a yearlong experimental treatment. It makes no sense for her not to be there with him. She's also homesick for the Midwest and a bit weary of the West. I'm not quite as tired of living out here, but I am aware of all the changes.

I find that long hair no longer means what it did, and with each passing year it's harder to tell the liberals from the rednecks. Gated communities separate the rich from the rest of us. Casinos have replaced meadows. Clear-cutting has chased the wild animals back into the high rock of so-called wilderness areas. Unceasing mountains of logs obscure the horizon in Idaho towns like Cascade and Pierce. The lack of employment opportunities is stifling.

So why don't I want to leave? Maybe because there are still parts of the West where you can't pick up a single radio station, and, when you're flying over them at night, not a single light shines below. I need the rush of loneliness I get when I look down from Galena Summit, along the foot-wide trickle of water that is the beginning of the Salmon River, and there is no sign of the modern world in any direction. Such grandeur can make you humble—or narcissistic.

My time here wasn't supposed to end. I had goals: to walk the Pacific Crest Trail; to live in an old adobe town in New Mexico; to see a cougar or a wolverine in the wild before I die. When I wrote my first bestseller, I was going to buy a little cabin and gather my grandchildren there each

Christmas in front of a roaring fire of tamarack. But none of this happened. I was too busy looking at the scenery and imagining living everywhere my eye landed. The truth is, you can't live in those isolated settings, unless you were born there or happen to be a relative of Ted Turner. "You have to arrive here with momentum," a buddy once told me about the West. He now owns a used-book store in Nashville. *Still, I think, no one moves back East. No one ever returns to Illinois. Do they?*

I could have spent the past twenty-five years in Telluride, Macon, Santa Fe, or Fayetteville, and it would have been pretty much the same. Or would it? The landscape draws us here, but we stay because of who we become. We tell ourselves the West is a great place to raise children. But is it a great place to raise adults?

All of my adult knowledge is shaped from living out West. I can tell how slick a road is just from looking at the snow. I know which hawthorns the long-eared owls hide in each December, and the difference in temperature between the hot springs at Lowman and at Pine Flats. I know Stanley, Idaho, has a population of sixty-nine; Durango, Colorado, has an altitude of 6,512 feet. Idaho's Kendrick grade is 9 percent, but I can make it all the way down without touching my brakes. The Nez Perce visitor center near Lapwai has the best bathrooms on Highway 95. (It features drum music and native chanting piped into the stalls.) I can show you how to sneak into Arches National Park without paying. The worst coffee is at the truck stop at Biggs, Oregon, and, until it closed, the best huckleberry pie used to be at Mom's Cafe at Syringa, Idaho.

So many things have changed in the last quarter century. And what precisely did I expect would happen? That I wouldn't get old? That my daughter wouldn't grow up and leave home quicker than wet soap out of your hand? That I could keep hiding from my relatives forever?

To add to my shame over admitting to Jake that I may end up back in my birth state, the Land of Lincoln, I woke up this morning—the morning of our camping trip—with a case of Bell's palsy. My face is twisted on one side like a Picasso painting. Anything I drink slides down my chin, and my winning smile is now a permanent sneer. One eye blinks like a cheap motel miniblind that won't close. People look away as if I were a madman. (A search on the Internet reveals more bad news: Some cases last for several years, and there are no special literary grants for writers with Bell's palsy.)

I blame vanity as the cause. *OK, God,* I think, *I won't suck in my cheeks anymore. No more flexing in the mirror. And I will never shave my back again (but I'm going to stay on those ear and nose hairs). Please, just give me back my face.* Not quite the Lord's Prayer, but heartfelt.

Jake and I eventually get rained out of the Bitterroots, but not before he talks me into taking the wrong fork in the trail, which leads us to a dead-end in a marsh called Big Stew, around 14 miles from the trailhead. A June sprinkle soon becomes a torrential downpour, soaking every inch of our belongings. We make camp next to a large group of bear hunters, who are all out looking for camp at the moment. The lone female cook, fearing rape and startled by my upside-down face, will not invite us inside her dry tent for a friendly cup of coffee. Yet another myth about the West— that folks here are neighborly—dies a painful death.

I finally do recite the Lord's Prayer (and mean it) in the gloom of my dripping tent, where I sit up all night in an inch of cold mountain water. Jake, hunkered down in his own sodden tent and shoveling back bee pollen and hard-boiled eggs, asks how I'm doing. "You don't want to know," I yell back through the storm, stuffing my last pair of dry socks inside my shirt next to my skin. My air mattress is an island. No sleep tonight.

Midwesterners always look at the West as a mythical get-away, a promised land where they can escape those humid July and August days. They look west beyond Iowa and imagine cowboys, Indians, and 5 percent humidity. To say to someone in Illinois that you live out West—in places like Missoula or Santa Fe—still gives you a special aura. But I am the only one I know from my old neighborhood who came West and stayed.

When I attended my twenty-fifth high school reunion in Chicago, my classmates—most of them well-heeled lawyers and doctors—looked at me as if I were a ghost. They gathered around, and some even touched my beat-up thrift-shop sports coat.

"We thought you had died."

"No," I said. "I just moved out West."

I have this nightmare in which I'm returning to the Midwest, and as I pull into town, everyone is hastily packing to move to Livingston and Telluride. The temperature is 98 degrees, and the humidity is 100 percent. They all look at me with disbelief, sweat dripping from the tips of their noses, and say, "You actually moved back to Illinois from the West? Why?"

Why indeed. I wonder each night while my wife rummages in the basement, sorting, discarding, and packing. Stacks of dusty books rise from the floor. "Do you want to keep this?" she asks, holding up a Hardy Boys mystery. Rugs are rolled up like giant burritos and tied with twine. Boxes appear. Furniture disappears. She visits a Realtor in Illinois.

"I'm sick of the West," she says with tears in her eyes. "I want to be in Illinois by the fall. I want to hold my father's hand."

As a giant hint, she hangs a poster titled "Spring Woodland Wildflowers of Illinois": blue cohosh, doll's eyes, redbud, Virginia waterleaf, bloodroot.

"What if I don't go with you?" I ask.

"I don't want you to do anything you don't want to do."

In the summer she replaces the spring poster with "Summer Prairie Wildflowers and Grasses of Illinois": compass plant, cordgrass, big bluestem, prairie dock, Illinois tick trefoil.

Realtors appraise the house while I'm out. I wake up each morning at three, terrified. *Damn, I forgot to see Glacier National Park!* So much landscape; so little time.

How do you know when you've stayed too long? How do you know when to leave? Time is running out. I am welcome to join her.

On our last trip to Illinois, we went bird-watching down the Great River Road, along the steamy Mississippi. Fireflies danced in the meadows, and all the birds were bright red and orange. I saw my first indigo bunting, a Peter Max shade of electric blue never seen in the West. From up on the bluffs, amid hardwoods I couldn't identify, we watched a boom of twenty barges coming up the river from the South, hauling corn, cotton, cars, and oil drums. I thought of one reason for moving there: We would be in the middle of the country, in the center of commerce instead of at the end of an economic cul-de-sac.

That evening, in the old French river town of Chester, I ate heaping platefuls of catfish, mashed potatoes, and fried chicken at a buffet where no one in the dining room weighed less than 300 pounds. *In a few years,* I thought, *will this be me?*

Late at night in the Big Stew with Jake, the bear hunters return on horseback. The sounds of hooves tripping over rocks and the scary voices of men echo through the empty valley. "How did they get in here?" they shout to each other through the rain. They turn their horses loose, and for the rest of the evening, the horses take turns galloping by our tents, snorting and farting, and generally disregarding our need for sleep.

In the morning, Jake, brave soul that he is, pays the men a visit to inquire as to just where the hell we are. I tell him to come and get me if they offer coffee, but otherwise he's on his own. I despise bear hunters, with their homicidal attitudes and their peanut-brained hounds. Jake returns—

without coffee, of course—and reports that the men are stunned that we actually walked all this distance in one day. The scent of bacon soon fills the little valley, replacing the stench of horse crap. I almost lose a filling on an oatmeal Power Bar. Jake eats more bee pollen and offers me some raisin-colored creek water spiked with iodine. I tell him I'd rather die of thirst.

We trudge off in poor spirits and wet, squeaky socks, cutting short our backpacking trip by a night. Rain continues to pelt us. All the way back down the mountain, we follow a trail of fresh bear tracks and discarded candy wrappers. (Snickers seems to be popular with hunters.) Soon, the path becomes a treacherous trough of mud and horse shit a foot and a half deep. Every now and then, I come across a confused snake and frog wondering how to cross the trail. Jake is having a horrible time in his K-Mart tennis shoes with Velcro straps. I debate whether or not to carry him out if he snaps his ankle. In my foul mood, I could go either way.

Finally, after eight hours, we arrive back at the trailhead just as the sun breaks through the gloom and the clouds retreat back north to Canada. We stop in the small town of Lowell, at a cafe whose walls are lined with a musty collection of animal heads. (I suggest that the owners add blue-tick hounds to the collection.) We are ravenous and each order a "wilderness burger," which makes good use of a quarter pound of cow and is topped off with two slices of bacon, cheddar cheese, and a slab of ham—curly fries included, with no extra charge for the grease. (All that's missing is a coupon for a thousand bucks off your first heart bypass.)

In the next booth sit four long-distance bicyclists, erect young studs in skintight, rainbow-colored stretch gear. They look in fantastic shape, like bony Rhodesian Ridgebacks after a successful lion hunt. The bicyclists stare at my lopsided face as I try unsuccessfully to cram the burger inside my crooked mouth. I stare back until they look away, and then I cut my burger into tiny, geriatric bites. For the first time in my life, I envy another person's youth and health. Jake doesn't notice any of this. He is too busy with his curly fries, his hands drenched in grease. He is ecstatic. I'm exhausted— physically tired for a change. I face four hours of driving (and five more weeks of Bell's palsy). Jake's got a big empty house waiting for him, where he'll stretch out on the floor, tune his Goodwill clock radio to the preseason Broncos game, and sleep straight through for twelve hours. *Maybe it is time to go home*, I think.

✿

MID-MAY, THE FOLLOWING SPRING, and Jan and I are leaving Malheur National Wildlife Refuge in eastern Oregon after three days of camping and bird-watching. I am driving a rental car across a spit of asphalt called The Narrows, between Harney and Malheur lakes. High water laps at the road: no room to pull off, no margin for error. Egrets calmly stalk the shallows, their sharp bills ready to strike at unsuspecting frogs. Grebes float by with their necks twisted back in a yoga-like pose.

Jan has resigned her job and is completely packed. Almost immediately after the experimental treatment was over, a second melanoma was found on her father's back. Time is running out.

This trip has had all the feel of a farewell tour: one last blast through our familiar western stomping grounds. For this last trip I chose the longest, slowest route imaginable. Rattlesnake Grade out of Asotin, Washington, past Fields Spring at the top, down the treacherous grade to the Grande Ronde River, where we stopped among the cliff swallows and quail to eat almonds, apples, and cheese. The only human activity we saw were cowboys moving Herefords on the grassy cliffs above. So steep is the contour of these finger canyons that I expected the cowboys, cows, and horses all to come tumbling down upon us. After lunch, we drove up a twisty ascent into northeastern Oregon. The snowcapped Wallowas rose above the town of Joseph, and to the east, across Snake River's Hell's Canyon, was a mirror of snow and peaks—the Seven Devils.

We've just been to our primary destination, a dead-end deep in the willows and cattails of Malheur. Avocets and burrowing owls were our goal, but looming over the entire trip like migrating turkey vultures was the specter of The Move.

I mention to Jan that this skinny, no-shoulder road is reminiscent of elevated freeway on the way from Chicago to Indiana. I remember riding that highway in the back seat of my mother's friend's Mustang convertible with the top down, Lake Michigan winds attacking me from all sides. I hid my head between my legs, terrified of being blown out of the car. That's how I learned to pray.

Almost immediately after I tell this story, the panic attack begins. No voices this time, but I can't get enough air. I feel faint and weak in the knees. High-desert wind, fresh water, shorebirds, and swift moving spring clouds call to me like sirens. I know if I give in, I'll wake up in a hospital.

"Jan, I feel funny." I slap my face and roll down the window. "Talk to me. Just keep talking."

"Do you want to pull over?" she asks, but there is no shoulder, only sky, water, and way too many coots. Her voice sounds as if it's coming to me through a tunnel. To keep from passing out, I tell Jan how the same feeling came over me in Boise last fall while I was driving in four lanes of rush-hour traffic. I describe the absurdity of an Idaho rush hour. Now I'm about to spin out into the briny waves of Lake Malheur.

Jan gently talks me through to the safety of sage on the other side. "Look, we're almost there," she says. "It's OK." Her calm, kind words and her hand on my leg to steady me are so overwhelmingly compassionate that at that moment I decide we belong together, forever, no matter where we end up.

Somehow I make it to the other side of the water, but I am rattled. What is happening to me?

As we continue our trip, I think, *Please, Jan, let's not bring up Illinois. Let's just soak up this one perfect spring week traveling through the West with the flocks of geese and cranes on the wing.*

In the sweet, lost towns of Lostine, Fox, and Wallowa, we make it our job to look for beauty in old-growth farmstead lilacs. Along the windy cottonwoods that feed from the rushing creeks of mountain runoff, we marvel (again) at how beautiful this country is. *Maybe*, I think, *just maybe, if I show her one more mountain range or one more sandstone canyon, I can win her over, convince her that we belong out here.*

Everything goes pretty well until Ukiah, a town the size of a placemat. The most attractive structure around is one of those overbuilt, modern U.S. Forest Service office-mansions. The rest of the town looks like a bad haircut. Gas is priced at extortion levels and comes with a long, poorly thought out antigovernment lecture from a man dressed in dirty overalls and his exhausted wife, whose T-shirt features the cast from the long-ago western sitcom *F Troop*. The gas station owner, who talks as if he has suffered more than a Kosovar Albanian, doesn't appreciate the government's insistence that he install a new, nonleaking underground gas tank at his own expense—$40,000. Looking off in the direction of the palatial Forest Service building, he proudly declares, "If I could chop the heads off all those bureaucrats, I would do it right here and now! I would love to see their heads rolling down Main Street."

My fragile brain does not care to imagine decapitations in this unfamiliar place, nor do I want Jan exposed to any more of this paranoid, rugged individualist western philosophy that comes from too much isolation and a lack of fresh produce. I especially do not want to remember *F Troop*. But I do; I remember every character, including the white actors who played the Indians.

For the remainder of the trip, we are spared anymore diatribes except, of course, my own. Illinois never comes up. In the intoxicating, soft days of spring, we hike, watch birds, and fall asleep to the cooing of cranes. We wear the sun in our faces and wonder in our expressions. I have the grandiose fantasy that I've just discovered the landscapes we're exploring. No one has ever seen Oregon's high desert the way I do.

Each day, we move through towns in which I once thought I might live. But you just don't arrive with your U-Haul in a blue-collar hamlet of four hundred and blend right in. Yet, all over the West, my boomer generation continues to attempt exactly that. Armed with our impending inheritances and preventive health care plans, our mission furniture, and our modems, we drop from the skies like NATO paratroopers in search of authentic small-town life and bargain-basement mortgages. And, before you know it, we're complaining about the development, the logging, the hunting, the farming, the lack of a good Internet connection, and the bad coffee and nondairy creamer served at the local cafe. We whine, worry, and fret. The sixties aside, we are not a happy-go-lucky generation. No wonder no one likes us. Hell, sometimes *I* don't even like us.

On our last night out, Jan and I stay at Ukiah-Dale State Park along Camas Creek, with its immense yellow pines, abundant fawn lilies, and wild parsley. We are the only campers here. In the dim twilight, we hurriedly set up the tent. Jan climbs in her bag and zips up against the chill. I light the lantern.

The campground host comes around to take down our

license plate number. A trim, shy cowboy of about sixty-five, he remembers us from when we passed through three days ago. He tells us we missed an afternoon snowstorm with a temperature of 22 degrees on May 8. "Pipes froze for a while," he says, shaking his head. After a few more minutes of weather talk, he relaxes and reveals that he's actually a fiddle player working at this campground until the Weiser, Idaho, fiddle festival begins in June: "For my first two numbers I'll play the 'Chinese Breakdown' and the 'Oklahoma Waltz.' Don't know yet about the third." For years, he tells us, he ran cattle "up and down in this Umatilla country," and his father was on the very last cattle drive out of Peter French's P Ranch in 1903. "They started in Burns and Harney City, picked up the P Ranch stock on their way south, and followed water all the way to Winnemuca. Took thirty-three days," he tells us. He says Peter French's grandson kept a cabin just up the road toward Pendleton, "but he just died." The cowboy looks down at his boots, his Oregon State Parks ball cap hiding his emotions. "Well, hope you don't get too cold," he says, and walks back toward his heated mobile home and his fiddle.

My earlier panic has subsided to a manageable level. I turn down the lantern, wiggle into my bag next to Jan, and kiss her goodnight.

"It helps keep me warm if you're touching me," she murmurs.

Jake, old man, I think as Jan hugs me, *you're missing out.* And I finally hear my own voice in my head, coming through clear and strong, and in the right octave. I shuffle the images of the past week: Wispy snow falling at the top of all four mountain passes from here to Malheur. Flocks of migrating curlews and white-faced ibises surrounding the runoff ponds in Burns. A hawk with terrible table manners devouring a toddler-sized jack rabbit. Two sandhill cranes fending off a stalking coyote. Great horned owlets on the verge of leaving home peering boldly out of their nest like messy ghosts. Pelicans swaying back and forth in a desert mirage. For an intoxicating second, I imagine I feel the vibrations under the tent from thousands of dusty cattle following water from Burns to Winnemuca. I listen for the cowboy's lone fiddle but instead hear a lost goose honking down the creek.

I fell in love with the West when I first saw the Rockies at the wet-ear age of seventeen, and here I go falling for her all over again. This time, though, it's a mature love from twenty-six years of living, loving, and fighting. Even with my crow's-feet, battle scars, and bad attitude, she always takes me back.

Tomorrow seems far away, next year an eternity. I try to imagine another place and another life, but I can't get beyond this moment, this perfect spring night. I feel victorious, the grateful recipient of a precious gift. I've been given one more night outside in the West, under stars, next to swift-moving waters. This is all I ever asked of her.

HALFWAY HOME

I'M AT THE HALFWAY POINT: 1,042 miles from northern Idaho, where I have lived for the past seventeen years. I'm on my way back to my native Illinois to begin the second half of my life. At this moment, my wife is getting settled in our new home, with our mismatched furniture and 126 boxes of stuff. We are returning to the Midwest to care for ill and aging parents, to create fresh memories with them, and to repay the unspoken debts we as children owe.

"Where is my home?" I ask myself at a rest stop on the Idaho–Utah border. "Where is my heart?" The two are separate now. Both answers come from the car radio in the form of a Gertrude Stein quote: "Do not fear the transition." Again, as at so many times in life, I am asked to be brave.

Many years ago, at the age of seventeen, influenced by John Denver singing about Rocky Mountain highs and Jack Kerouac writing about a life of poetry and adventure on the road, I abandoned my Illinois roots and headed west. I was part of a modern-day pioneer migration, only instead of Conestoga wagons, we traveled in Volkswagen microbuses, or by our thumbs. I rode in other people's cars, smug in my self-inflicted poverty, gazing at mountains and weird rock formations and listening to Gram Parsons sing, "'Cause I headed west to grow up with the country / Across those prairies with those waves of grain." I believed in that myth, along with others of my own creation, never realizing that one day I'd feel another kind of hunger and longing, one whose peaks and canyons wouldn't be big enough to satisfy. Suddenly (yes, it feels that quick) I am a grown-up with a profession, a college-age daughter, and decades of experience that didn't in the slightest resemble what Denver, Kerouac, or Parsons wrote about.

Although this move fulfills a powerful moral obligation—to become reconnected with family—I am dragging my feet. How hard it is to abandon one's history, even if it began as myth. To me, a twenty-seven-year veteran of six western states—not to mention a dismal earning record and severe frostbite—returning east feels like a defeat, a large crack in my identity. If I am no longer a westerner, what am I? Maybe the answer lies a thousand miles in front of me.

At the age of forty-four, I am also halfway (if all goes well and I continue to wear my bicycle helmet) through my time on earth. Writer Edward Abbey viewed each decade of his life as a day of the week. He assumed we all had about seventy years, or one "week," of high-quality living, although many people now live until the following Tuesday. By Abbey's reckoning, my current age places me at midday on Thursday, with the weekend looming not far ahead. And weekends go by faster than weekdays. Whatever I need to accomplish—correctly identifying every warbler; reading *Moby Dick*—it will have to be in the next three days.

Today I drove from nine in the morning until eight at night. In western Utah, I passed massive turkey ranches and coiled rattlers baking on the hot asphalt. I frequented McDonald's for bathroom stops because of their antimicrobial soap and generic cheeriness. I listened to sports talk radio and tried to understand why there were so many homeruns hit this season. Is the ball "juiced," or are the hitters just stronger? On *Ag in the Morning*, the host announced eagerly, "Today we're going to talk about hay!" And we did. Then Dr. Laura cackled like a gleeful witch at a single mother's trauma, and Rush Limbaugh sounded off about one thing or another. I drove through the worst traffic in Salt Lake City, where transportation engineers were busy ripping up the freeways. Salt Lake City is not my home, I was happy to note.

Tonight my home is a tent whose thin nylon walls provide little sense of security. The spring wind is working its way up the base of the La Sal Mountains and making its presence known. The radio reports that forty-two thousand babies were born on this day in India, bringing the population of that country to one billion. Forty-two thousand is enough to fill a small city. I imagine an entire city of babies—babies going to work at software companies; babies talking politics over tea; babies reading newspapers; babies jogging behind racing strollers; babies directing the traffic; wall-to-wall babies on the sidewalks.

Where I am camping tonight, there are no babies to be seen or heard, only a retired German couple who are touring the Americas in a VW van. I've been avoiding them because I want this trip to revolve around my own thoughts. Since I began this journey, I have hardly talked to anyone, just thank-yous to cashiers and short orders given to short-order cooks.

I have left my own baby, my twenty-year-old daughter, back in Idaho. This is the first time we will live so far from each other. She wants no part of moving to Illinois, although I extended the invitation. The night before I left, I went over to her one-room downtown apartment with a goodbye card and a Hallmark refrigerator magnet that expressed better than I was able a father's love for his daughter. I wore sunglasses to hide my tears when I handed her the card. I knew I was supposed to say something profound, but I couldn't think past my sorrow. She glanced quickly at the card and the magnet but didn't cry. "Let's go get pitas and watch a video," she suggested, defusing the tension.

She chose *Being John Malkovich*, a movie about entering another person's mind and seeing the world through different eyes—something I've wanted to do at certain moments in my life. My daughter and I sat together on her old couch, staring at the TV and playing with her orange kitten, neither of us knowing what the other was feeling.

All I can think now is that, with a new job and plenty of long-term friends and her dad soon to be a comfortable fifteen hundred miles away . . . well, my daughter is just getting to the good part.

Down the road from my campsite, in Moab, Utah, the streets are crowded with braless, tan, skinny women in Lycra shorts and Teva sandals, and loud, goateed aggressive men with their caps turned backward, which I guess suggests a rowdy, against-the-grain attitude. Twenty-seven years ago, I, too, came to Moab looking for adventure. At the beginning of my adult life and full of lofty, unsubstantiated opinions about the world, I wore beads and a ringed jacket and a flat-brimmed leather hat because Neil Young did, and I wrote down all my observations in a small red book because Kerouac did that too. Back then, Moab was just another sleepy Mormon town with watery coffee, uranium cowboys, and 3.2 percent beer. Now it's an athletic marinade of muscle and youth, committed to biking, climbing, hiking, four-wheeling, rafting, kayaking, swimming, and drinking exotic coffee blends. They are attractive to look at, these young people, as they exercise and preen against the red rock backdrop, but the speed and noise of this generation of adventurers are too much for me. Driving the narrow Colorado River Road, I felt pushed from behind by four-by-four pickups bristling with bike racks and bumper stickers denouncing the oil industry. *What is the hurry?* I thought.

I'm trying to enjoy this trip despite my intermittent anxiety over the disruption of moving and the dangers of traveling alone. *Enjoy this moment*, I advise myself, as if I'm two separate beings, one more stable than the other. *Don't regret not reading or hiking more. Don't worry about the past. You are a good parent.* But the loaded questions persist: How, precisely, have I been passing the years? Can I remember what I did in, say, 1991? Was 1993 a good year, and, if so, why? What, exactly, have I been doing for the past two decades? Only a few touchstones pop out: Raising a daughter, certainly, and establishing a career in writing. Divorce filled up a few sad years with weight gain and sloth. And now I'm in a new marriage that is too sweet for words.

I'd planned for this trip back to my home state of Illinois to be about taking stock at midlife. The world moves with such velocity that sometimes I have to sit still and remind myself that this stillness is actually my life: *Oh, so this is my life. I get it now. Hey, this feels good, this living in the moment.* But that epiphany soon fades, and I'm back to chewing on my nails and pulling out my eyebrow hairs one at a time, remembering some ancient hurt or chance not taken. *Now, what was it that felt so good a minute ago?*

Unlike twenty-seven years ago, when I lived life mostly in the future, I now sift through the past, trying to slow the galloping pace of time. How have I evolved between my seventeenth and forty-fourth years, my time out West? What shook out, and what stuck? Alone hour upon hour, my mind wants to play an endless loop of regret: missed opportunities, inadequate parenting, and loss of self.

I'm noticing a more labored quality to my step lately. I no longer glide along like the twenty-year-olds I saw on the trail today in Moab. I remarked to a fellow hiker that I'd hiked in that same canyon more than two decades ago. Looking up at the ancient slabs of rock, I said to him,

"Everything looked exactly the same." I was trying for a joke, but he didn't laugh. "Things don't change that much here," he said, trying for wisdom.

But we change, of course, even in our relationship to landscapes. In 1973, did I notice—*really* notice—the twisted bark of the oak trees, the leathery texture of the segment grass, or the flickering brilliance of the penstemon? I doubt it. More likely, I was trying to strike a pose, to affect an image I thought was original but was actually stolen from an album cover or a movie. Today my vanity has diminished. With the thick fog of adolescence lifted, I see clearly my remaining days and wonder how I will fill them up.

Out of all my stops and starts, two passions remain: writing and playing music. All that journal writing, as banal as it was, developed a muscle that led to a way of living in and interpreting this world. And all that guitar practice—figuring out songs, mastering the tricky barre chords, and finally achieving the alternating bass—that amounted to something, too. Neither has led to fame and fortune, but, if nothing else, poetry and song are agreeable ways to pass the time. More than that, the journals and the fingerpicking amount to a sort of spiritual retirement account, with compounded interest in creativity.

On this spring evening in the Utah desert, I spot a falling star and listen to the evening birds' songs announcing the close of a long day. East-facing cliffs glow in the last vestiges of scarlet light. As the winds die down, a nearby creek grows louder. Above, bats circle and dive. Soon the nighthawks and coyotes will start to call. It's not a bad life here at the halfway point; not bad at all to live in the present tense, to fall into the arms of a May evening in the desert. The second half of my life is beginning, and there is not much left for me to accomplish except to pay attention to and be generous toward this world. *I will notice everything*, I vow, as I start to drift off. *No matter where I am. Moment by moment. Everything.*

ABOUT THE AUTHOR

S TEPHEN J. LYONS IS THE AUTHOR OF *Landscape of the Heart*. His articles, essays, and reviews have appeared in many publications, including *Newsweek*, the *Washington Post*, *Salon*, *USA Today*, *Sierra*, and the *Sun*. After thirty years of living out West, he now lives in his native state of Illinois.